Ken Libbrecht's
Field Guide to
SNOWFLAKES

by Kenneth Libbrecht

Voyageur Press

Acknowledgments

Special thanks to Walter Tape, John Jaszczak, Valerie Pegg, and the staff at the North Adventure Inn for their hospitality during several snowflake photography expeditions.

Additional thanks to Alanna Libbrecht and Rachel Wing for preliminary editing.

First published in 2006 by Voyageur Press, an imprint of Quarto Publishing Group USA Inc., 400 First Avenue North, Suite 400, Minneapolis, MN 55401 USA

Voyageur Press titles are also available at discounts in bulk quantity for industrial or sales-promotional use. For details write to Special Sales Manager at Quarto Publishing Group USA Inc., 400 First Avenue North, Suite 400, Minneapolis, MN 55401 USA

To find out more about our books, join us online at www.voyageurpress.com.

Library of Congress Cataloging-in-Publication Data

Libbrecht, Kenneth George.
  Ken Libbrecht's field guide to snowflakes / by Kenneth Libbrecht.
      p. cm.
  Includes index.
  ISBN-13: 978-0-7603-2645-9 (printed laminated cover)

  1. Snowflakes--Juvenile literature. 2. Snowflakes--Pictorial
works--Juvenile literature. I. Title.
  QC926.32L529 2006
  551.57'841--dc22

                        2006016357

Editor: Leah Noel
Designer: Jennifer Bergstrom
Printed in China

On the cover: *(Main and bottom left and center)* Stellar plates, the type of crystals that give falling snow its sparkle. *(Bottom right)* A stellar dendrite with large leaf-shaped branches.

On the frontispiece: A stellar dendrite with sidebranches full of ridges.

On the back cover: *(Top)* A stunning stellar plate crystal, which fell in a late-night snowfall. *(Middle)* A stellar dendrite with imperfect symmetry. *(Bottom)* A twelve-branched star snowflake.

Contents

Snowflake Watching

This book is about snowflake watching—taking a close look at those remarkable ice sculptures that drift down from the clouds. You've probably heard that no two snowflakes are alike, and you may have occasionally glanced down at the sparkling crystals on your sleeve, but have you ever seen fernlike stellar dendrites, sectored plates, twelve-branched stars, or the always-bizarre capped columns? If not, then read on, and look more closely during the next snowfall. You may be amazed by what you find.

As hobbies go, snowflake watching is easy, inexpensive, and a simple pleasure for young and old alike. All you really need (besides a cold climate and a good field guide) is a low-cost fold-up magnifier. Keep it tucked away in your coat pocket and use it whenever the falling crystals look interesting. Every snowfall is different, and many will not produce great snowflakes, but sometimes the displays are simply gorgeous.

Snowflake watching is similar to bird watching in many respects. Both activities take you outdoors, searching for inconspicuous treasure, and both give you a better sense of the natural world. It's true that bird watching can be done on a warm summer day, while snowflake watching takes place in the cold of winter. But a snowflake watcher will never be bothered by mosquitoes!

Looking at snowflakes is a much underappreciated recreation, in my opinion. Personally, I find that the endless variety of forms and patterns is always fascinating to observe, and pulling out your magnifier is definitely a conversation-starter on the chairlift. Yet there are probably a million bird watchers out there for every snowflake watcher. Why is that? It's not the cold, as there are plenty of other popular winter activities. It's not the equipment, since so little is needed. And it's certainly not the lack of beautiful snowflakes. Perhaps what's been missing is a good field guide.

It is my sincere hope that this small book will motivate more potential snowflake watchers by showing what's out there waiting to seen. The Lilliputian world of snowflakes is revealed here to pique your curiosity, so that perhaps you too will pause to examine—and ponder—these dazzling ice masterpieces.

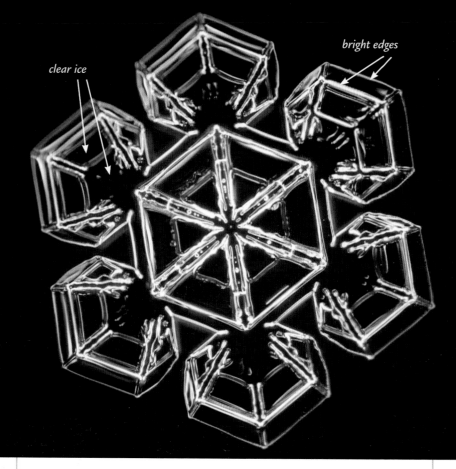

clear ice

bright edges

Case Study 1: White Snow. Throughout this book, I will examine individual snowflakes up close, presenting a number as case studies of various particular characteristics. The above photograph, for example, shows a snowflake as you might see it on your sleeve (provided you are wearing black). Although you may have thought snowflakes were white, if you look carefully, you will find that many are transparent, like glass. In the above example, you can readily see the black background through the clear ice.

Mostly what you see in the picture are the various edges because these scatter the most light. Snowflakes and snowbanks look white because you see light scattered from all the edges; it's the same white you see on a surface of scratched or etched glass.

Most of the pictures in this book were taken by shining colored light through the crystals from behind. The ice then refracts the light like a very complex lens, giving a much better view of each snowflake's internal structure.

Part I

UNDERSTANDING SNOWFLAKES

Snowflake Fundamentals

Let's begin by taking a close look at what snowflakes are and how they are created. In doing so, you'll better understand why snowflakes have such complex shapes, how their various patterns arise, and the origin of their sixfold symmetry.

Observing and understanding often go hand in hand when examining of snowflakes. Armed with an understanding of their inner workings, you'll notice many subtle details in their structure. In turn, as you observe the characteristics of different snowflakes, you can better understand their formation. Snowflake watching is always enjoyable, but the activity is enhanced when you know something about how their beautiful shapes and patterns arise.

The first thing to know about snowflakes is that they are made of ordinary ice. Yet they are not frozen raindrops, nor do they form from liquid water; snowflakes are created when ice condenses directly from water *vapor* in the air. As you will see, the dynamics of the condensing vapor are what give snowflakes their distinctive appearance.

Ice is a crystalline material, which means that the water molecules are arranged in a regular lattice. Even when a snow crystal has a complex shape, its water molecules are aligned throughout its entire construction.

A *snow crystal* refers to a single crystal of ice, like the one pictured above. The term *snowflake* can refer to a single snow crystal, but it can also mean an agglomeration of many snow crystals that floats to earth as a flimsy puff-ball.

Many of the features visible in snowflakes—their sixfold symmetry, their facets, and the orientation of the different branches and sidebranches—result from the ordered placement of molecules in the ice lattice.

In order to understand how snow crystals get their striking shapes, you need to understand how water molecules in the air attach to a growing crystal. Nature does not pattern a snowflake by removing material from a block of ice, but rather by selectively adding to the crystal via condensation. How this all works is the subject of Part I of this book.

The Morphology Diagram

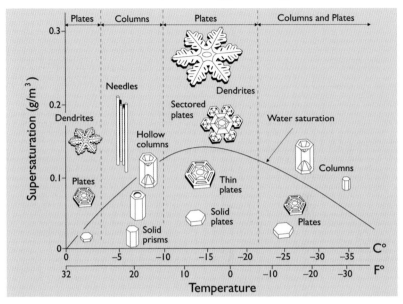

An important insight into snow-flakes comes from looking at what types of crystals grow at different temperatures and at different humidity levels, which is shown graphically above in what is called the *snow crystal morphology diagram*.

Note how the overall crystal shapes change dramatically with temperature. Thin, plate-like crystals grow when the weather is just below freezing, while slender columns and needles form when it's a few degrees colder. Especially large and photogenic plates appear when the temperature is around –15° C (5° F), while smaller plates and columns develop in somewhat colder conditions. The morphology diagram also shows that complex, branched crystals appear when the humidity is high, while low humidity levels yield simpler, faceted crystals.

Why snow crystals grow this way is something of a scientific puzzle. Nevertheless, as you look in detail at snowflakes, the morphology diagram is an invaluable tool for interpreting the overall shapes of different crystal types.

> Humidity is displayed above in terms of the *supersaturation*, or excess water vapor in the air. Zero supersaturation means the humidity is 100 percent, at which point the air is said to be *saturated*. The *water saturation* line in the diagram gives the humidity level found in dense winter clouds.

Snowflake Symmetry

Two questions quickly arise when looking at snowflakes: *1)* Why are they all so different? and *2)* How does the growth of all six arms become coordinated? The crystal above, for example, has a shape that is complex and quite unique from all others. In addition, you can clearly see how the various sidebranches and markings are nearly identical on each main arm. What causes a snowflake to grow this way?

The answer can in part be found in the morphology diagram, which shows that snow crystal formation is very sensitive to local conditions. If you consider the life of a snowflake, you find that its shape is determined by the history of its growth. As it blows about inside the clouds, a developing crystal experiences ever-changing temperatures and humidity levels along the way. Each change in its local environment causes a change in the way the crystal grows. After numerous twists and tumbles, the final structure can be quite complex. And since no two snowflakes follow exactly the same path, no two are exactly alike.

But while different snowflakes follow different paths, the six arms of an individual crystal travel together. Thus, the six arms grow in synchrony, simply because they each experience the same growth history.

However, there are many ways to spoil a snowflake's symmetry. Defects in the crystal lattice can happen; crowding from neighbors may impede growth; and there is the potential for midair collisions with other crystals and cloud droplets. These are all common occurrences, and each will result in asymmetrical growth.

Don't let the photographs in this book fool you into thinking that all snowflakes are precisely symmetrical. If you look for yourself during a typical snowfall, you will quickly discover that such ideal specimens are rare. When photographing snowflakes, I sometimes sift through them by the thousands to find the most outstanding examples. Symmetry is inherent in snow crystals, but it is fragile and never perfect.

Common lore says that no two snowflakes are alike, but is this really true? If you could somehow sift through every snowflake on the planet, wouldn't you find at least a few duplicates?

To answer this, first consider how many ways you can arrange the books on your bookshelf. If you have, say, fifteen books, then there are fifteen choices for the first book, fourteen for the second, thirteen for the third, and so on. If you multiply it out, you will find there are over a trillion ways to arrange just fifteen books. With 100 books, the number of possible arrangements is vastly greater than the total number of atoms in the entire universe!

Now consider how many ways nature can arrange the markings on a snowflake. With a complex specimen, you might easily count a hundred or more individual features, each of which could go in a different place. The math is like that with the books, so the number of possible ways to make a snowflake is absurdly large. Thus, the probability of finding two identical specimens is essentially zero, even if you looked at every one ever made.

Of course, this reasoning applies to complex crystals with lots of markings. Simpler crystals have fewer features, so there are fewer possible arrangements. The simplest possible snowflake is a hexagonal plate, which

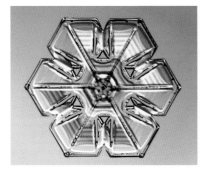

has only a length and a width, and such simple crystals can look alike.

The pictures above show two snow crystals that are similar but not identical. They fell within minutes of one another, and it's apparent they traveled together through the clouds. Both have the same overall shape, and many of their markings are similar as well. If you just glance at them, you might think they are two pictures of the same crystal. But if you examine them closely, comparing the two in detail, you can find many differences. With snowflakes, the question of similarity depends on how carefully you look.

Case Study 2: Exceptional Symmetry. Occasionally a snow crystal will exhibit an especially precise sixfold symmetry, as in the specimen shown above. If you look carefully, you can see that even most of the minor markings are reproduced with good fidelity six times around the crystal. I took this photograph early one January morning in Fairbanks, Alaska, when the temperature was a brisk –18° C (0° F) and the crystal facets were sharp. The crystal measures about 2 mm (0.08 inches) from tip to tip.

Smaller, simpler, faceted crystals like this one tend to be more symmetrical than larger, complex, branched ones. Slower growth is generally more stable and produces smaller, more symmetrical crystals.

main branches

sidebranches

Case Study 3: Imperfect Symmetry. The above photograph shows the kind of imperfect snowflake symmetry you more typically find on your sleeve. You can see that the six main branches are not quite the same length, plus the sidebranches are unevenly placed with somewhat random sizes. This specimen is about 1.5 times larger than the previous one, and its rapid, branched growth resulted in a less symmetrical form.

In spite of its complex shape, you can still tell that this is a single crystal of ice. Note how the branches and sidebranches are all oriented at 60-degree angles relative to one another. This is an indicator of the underlying order of the molecular lattice.

Crystal Faceting

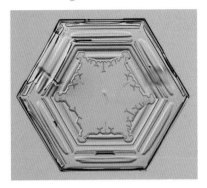

Snow crystals often show many flat crystalline surfaces, or *facets*. Bright reflections off these mirror-like facets give freshly fallen snow its sparkle, and you can easily see individual sparkles when you examine snowflakes on your sleeve.

The growth of facets is one of the most important mechanisms for producing the different shapes and patterns seen in snowflakes. Faceting is also the process by which the geometry of the water molecule is transferred to the geometry of a large snow crystal.

Crystals form facets because some crystalline surfaces accumulate material more slowly than others. You can see how this works by considering the growth of an initially round grain of ice, shown on the left side of the diagram below. The crystal grows when water molecules in the air condense on its surface. Molecules

are especially attracted to the atomic-scale nooks and crannies because of the extra molecular binding there. The flat areas, by contrast, have fewer dangling chemical bonds and are thus less favorable attachment sites.

As condensing water molecules jockey into position, they tend to fill in the molecular rough spots quickly. After the ice grain has been growing for a while, only the flat surfaces remain. Thus the crystal eventually becomes faceted, regardless of its initial shape.

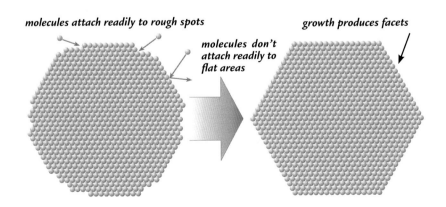

molecules attach readily to rough spots

molecules don't attach readily to flat areas

growth produces facets

The molecular latticework in an ice crystal yields two main types of facets: six prism facets plus two basal facets, as illustrated at right. The shape bounded by these eight planes is called a *hexagonal prism*. Extremely tiny snow crystals often have this shape, or something close to it, as do crystals that grow very slowly.

Faceting is a guiding force in snowflake growth even when it does not produce perfectly flat facets. Large stellar (i.e., star-shaped) crystals, for example, are flat because of basal faceting. Water molecules attach readily to the prism surfaces,

A hexagonal ice prism

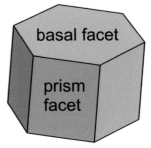

basal facet

prism facet

but hardly at all to the basal surfaces. Thus the edges grow out rapidly to form thin plates of ice. Even when you add patterns and branches, the overall crystal shape remains that of a thin, flat plate.

Snowflake symmetry always derives from the hexagonal ice lattice via faceting. Whenever you see a sixfold symmetrical snow crystal, you know it must have experienced faceted growth at some point in its history. Snow crystals are usually faceted when they are very small, and they often show remnants of this near their centers, as seen below.

Side view of a plate-like crystal

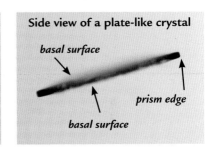

basal surface

prism edge

basal surface

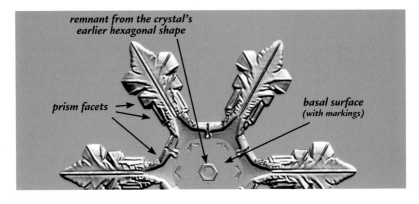

remnant from the crystal's earlier hexagonal shape

prism facets →

basal surface (with markings)

The Branching Instability

Branching is another fundamental concept in the creation of snowflakes, as this is how complex shapes arise. Without branching, snow crystals would be rather uninteresting, appearing mostly like simple hexagonal prisms. The branching instability provides a natural explanation for how beautifully elaborate snow crystal structures can appear spontaneously from nothing more than freezing water vapor.

To see how this process works, consider the growth of an initially flat ice surface, shown in the top diagram at right. For growth to occur, water molecules must diffuse through the air and condense onto the ice surface. When the surface is flat, molecules diffuse down and attach themselves with no preference in position. Thus, the whole surface advances upward uniformly.

But if a small bump appears on the surface, as shown in the second panel, then molecules will diffuse more readily to the top of the bump. In effect, this protrusion sticks out farther into the supersaturated air, accumulating material at a slightly higher rate. This means the bump grows a bit faster than its surroundings. After a while, it becomes even more pronounced, causing it to grow faster still.

This positive feedback is why the effect is called an *instability*. Minute features will inevitably grow larger,

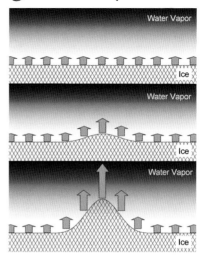

so the growth of a flat surface is *unstable*. Bumps eventually appear and grow into branches, followed by sidebranches and other patterns. Complexity arises spontaneously because of this instability, as long as the crystal is growing. The branching instability exists because the speed of snow crystal growth is limited by the slow diffusion of water molecules through the air. Different regions on a crystal "compete" for the available water vapor supply. More water vapor causes faster growth. Rapidly growing areas, like the tips of branches, use up the water vapor before it has a chance to diffuse to the inner regions. The competition for water vapor and the branching instability that results from it are ever-present themes in snow crystal growth.

Faceting versus Branching

Faceting and branching are the two dominant forces in snow crystal growth, pulling in opposite directions. Faceting is a stabilizing process that drives the formation of flat surfaces and simple shapes. In contrast, branching is an unstable process that takes simple shapes and makes them complex. Snow crystals are sculpted by the interplay of these two forces.

Consider the transition from faceted to branched growth, shown in the diagram below. For small crystals (stage 1), faceting dominates because the diffusion distances are short. Thus, the crystal takes the form of a simple hexagonal prism.

As the prism grows larger, it enters stage 2, where diffusion plays a greater role, bringing more molecules to the corners than to the facet centers. The corners respond by growing out slightly, which immediately makes the facet surfaces just a bit concave.

This deviation from perfect flatness means that there are more available molecular bonds at the facet centers than at the corners. A dynamical equilibrium quickly establishes itself, in which diffusion brings more molecules to the corners, but the molecules stick more readily to the rougher centers. The two effects automatically balance to give uniform growth across each facet.

Entering stage 3, the facets become even more concave, and the density of bonds at the facet centers increases until the surface is rough and the dynamical equilibrium breaks down. Then the centers can no longer keep up with the corners, and the branching instability kicks in. At that point, branches sprout and grow out from the corners.

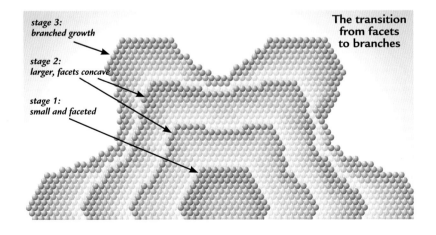

stage 3:
branched growth

stage 2:
larger, facets concave

stage 1:
small and faceted

The transition from facets to branches

Even after the transition to branching has occurred, faceting continues to affect snow crystal growth. Under the right conditions, faceting can even direct the formation of new branches, in a process called *induced sidebranching*.

The diagram below shows a series of events that will induce a set of sidebranches on a growing snowflake. The left side of the diagram shows the tip of one of the six primary branches of a stellar snow crystal. At this stage, the humidity around the crystal happens to be high, so the growth is fast and the tip is rounded. Water molecules are striking the surface in such great numbers that they accumulate on flat and rough surfaces alike, negating the formation of prism facets. Thus, the tip grows out rapidly and the arm becomes longer.

Then the crystal happens to fall into a region of lower humidity, which slows the growth rate. Slower growth favors faceting, so the tip becomes less rounded and more angular in form. After a while at low humidity, facets develop with sharp corners, as is shown in the middle part of the diagram.

At this point, the crystal happens to tumble into another region of high humidity, which increases the growth rate once again. Since the facet corners now stick out, the branching instability causes new branches to sprout, as shown on the right side of the diagram.

Although only one primary branch is shown, the same humidity variations occur on the other branches as well. The end result is a set of induced sidebranches that are symmetrically placed on each of the six arms.

This confluence of events may seem unusual, but remember that the humidity seen by a crystal is changing all the time. Induced sidebranching events are actually quite common and are another important example of the interplay between the two primary forces of faceting and branching.

Induced sidebranching

fast growth
rounded tips

slower growth
facets form

fast growth
branches form

The Knife-Edge Instability

One thing you don't immediately realize from pictures is just how thin snowflakes can be. A typical stellar crystal might easily have a thickness 100 times smaller than its diameter. Looking at a branch from the side, as in the picture at right, you begin to see that the edge of a snow crystal can be as sharp as a knife.

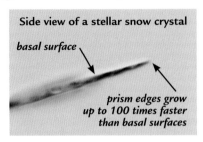

Side view of a stellar snow crystal

basal surface

prism edges grow up to 100 times faster than basal surfaces

Even more remarkably, many plate-like snow crystals have thicknesses of about 0.01 mm (0.0004 inches), regardless of diameter. That's roughly ten times thinner than a sheet of paper. Not all snowflakes are this thin, but enough are that you know something about the crystal growth process tends to produce this particular thickness.

A different growth mechanism is required to explain why plates become so thin, which I call the *knife-edge instability*. For reasons that are not well understood, the molecular dynamics of crystal growth actually change at a sharp edge, in such a way as to greatly accelerate the edge growth. Again, there is a positive feedback that is the hallmark of an instability. Forming a sharp edge increases its growth, which then sharpens the edge even more.

When the humidity is low, the knife-edge instability is not triggered. Then plates are thicker, as seen in the morphology diagram. If you slowly turned up the humidity while watch-ing a crystal grow, you would find that not much happened until you reached some threshold value. Then the instability would suddenly kick in and the edge would taper down quickly. From then on, the plate would grow outward without getting appreciably thicker.

The knife-edge instability is a rather esoteric bit of crystal physics, but it's quite important for the growth of snowflakes. We'll see it often when we look at the different snow crystal types in detail. Without the knife-edge instability, snow crystals would be smaller, thicker, and blockier, lacking many of their most beautiful characteristics.

induced
sidebranches

remnant
hexagonal
prism

Case Study 4: Branching and Sidebranching. The above snowflake started out as a small hexagonal prism, and you can still see a remnant outline of this simple form near the center of the crystal. The six primary branches sprouted from the corners of this small hexagon.

Initially the arms grew out as straight twigs, without any sidebranches. Then the crystal experienced a strong induced sidebranching event when the arms were about one-third of their final length. If you look carefully, you can still see some residual faceting where the sidebranches sprouted. A few weaker sidebranching events occurred later, when the arms were about two-thirds of their final length, but the sidebranching then was only partially symmetrical.

If you stare at this crystal for a while, you can begin to imagine its growth history. First, the simple prism; then, with twig-like branches; then, a symmetrical set of sidebranches; then, additional sidebranches; and finally, the shape you see here. At each stage, the growth was determined by the local weather conditions around the crystal.

induced
sidebranches

Case Study 5: More Branching and Sidebranching. The above example is similar to the previous one. Both are thin-branched stellar crystals showing several induced sidebranching events. Both formed around the special temperature of -15° C (5° F), as shown in the morphology diagram.

In the above picture, you cannot see the original hexagonal prism, but it must have been there to guide the formation of the six main arms. The arms started growing as straight twigs, but soon the humidity started fluctuating rather erratically, probably as the crystal dropped through different cloud layers. The changing conditions produced a whole series of induced sidebranching events, most of which occurred symmetrically on the six arms.

I found both these crystals in northern Ontario, near the town of Cochrane, which is one of my favorite spots for photographing snowflakes. This region has long, snowy winters without much wind, making it popular with snowmobilers as well. The temperature at this location is quite variable throughout the winter season, producing an especially rich variety of different snow crystal types.

Ridges, Ribs, and Rims

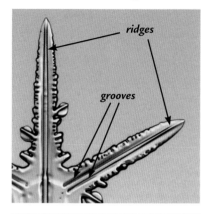

ridges

grooves

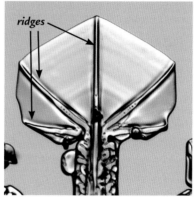

ridges

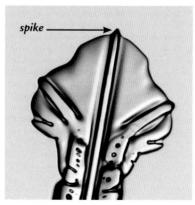

spike

The basal faces of snow crystals are usually decorated with ornate patterns, and you can identify a few recurring design elements. Complex arrangements are largely made from variations and combinations of these few basic features.

Ridges are linear markings, like spines, that often appear on snow crystal branches. The top picture on the left shows two branches with ridges running down their centers. Near the tips, the features look like simple linear bumps, while farther down they become flanked by two parallel grooves. In many crystals, you can find double-groove markings that are quite pronounced.

Ridges always originate at the corners where two prism facets meet. The plate in the center picture, which sits at the end of a branch, is marked with five linear features, one running from each facet corner. Note that as a plate grows, its ridges leave a record of where the corners were at previous times. If the facet corners don't trace out straight lines as the crystal grows, then the ridges will become curved.

Sometimes ridges have an accentuated appearance, as in the third picture. While it was growing, this plate looked essentially like the one above it. Later, the thin edges of the plate evaporated away more quickly than the thicker spine. As a result, a spike sticks out beyond the plate.

Ribs are linear features of a different nature that look a bit like hexagonal tree rings on snow crystals. The top picture on the right, for example, displays a series of concentric hexagons on the face of the crystal. The picture below it shows a more subtle sequence of hexagons on its surface.

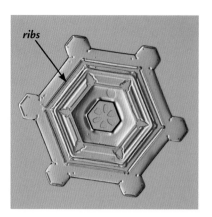

These lines are remnants of growth changes that occurred over the life of the crystal, much like tree rings. For example, changes in humidity cause the edge of a plate to change its thickness, driven by the dynamics of the knife-edge instability. If the edge alternates between thick and thin as it grows outward, a series of ribs will be imprinted in the ice.

Rims are what I call these same features when they appear on the outer borders of plates, as shown in the middle photograph at right. Thick rims are fairly common because the humidity usually drops during the last phases of growth, as a snow crystal falls below the clouds. The lower humidity yields a thicker edge, and, hence, a thick rim.

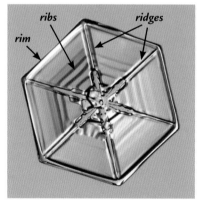

Ribs and rims can also frequently be found on the branches of many snow crystals, as in the third picture, where they form line segments instead of complete hexagons.

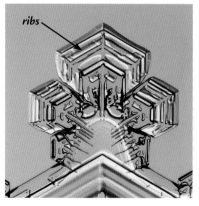

Ribs, rims, and ridges account for much of the intricate patterning seen in many different types of snowflakes.

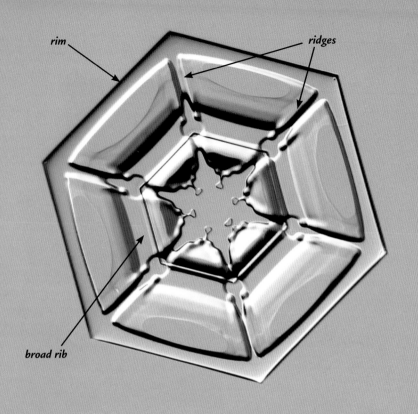

rim

ridges

broad rib

Case Study 6: Ridges, Ribs, and Rims. This small hexagonal plate shows all three of these design elements. The plate started out as a faceted hexagonal prism, as most plates do. Ridges formed at the corners when the plate was tiny, and the ridge growth changed with time as the crystal moved about, which resulted in the somewhat flowery pattern near the center.

When the crystal was about half its final size, the humidity dropped and the edge of the plate thickened as it grew. After a short while, the humidity increased again and the edge thinned, leaving behind a fairly broad rib in the process. Then the crystal fell into a region of low humidity during the last phases of its growth, producing a thick rim around its outer perimeter.

This specimen is just over a millimeter (0.04 inches) in diameter, hardly more than a speck when seen with the naked eye. Even a good magnifier will not reveal these features, so a microscope is needed to make out the details. As you can see, taking a close look has its rewards. One of the great pleasures in finding and photographing snowflakes is that even the most inconsequential crystal is decorated with its own elaborate pattern.

Sublimation

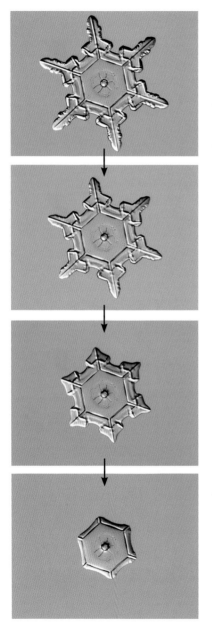

Soon after a snowflake leaves its cloudy nursery, it stops growing and begins to evaporate away in a process called sublimation. The ice does not melt into liquid, but goes directly into the gas phase, just the opposite of a growing crystal. The process will be fast or slow depending on the surrounding temperature and humidity. Sublimation can dramatically alter a snowflake's shape, often in just minutes.

The photos on the left show a crystal slowly evaporating away under the bright lights of my microscope over a period of about five minutes. Sublimation always removes the more delicate outer structures first—the parts that stick out the most. The arms shorten, sharp facets become rounded, and details disappear. The trend is always toward simpler, smoother shapes.

Some snow crystals sublimate quite a lot even before they reach the ground, arriving with a partially melted appearance. These travel-worn specimens can look very different from when they were in the clouds.

The same is true for snowflakes that have been on the ground a while. The crystals in a snowbank almost never show the sharp facets and intricate markings found in freshly fallen snow. Sublimation is an enemy of snowflake watchers, since it renders the crystals rather dull and featureless, erasing the beautiful patterns that existed during their growth.

Rime

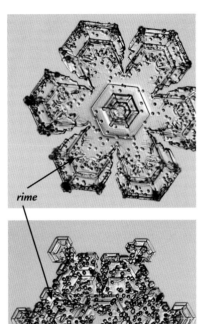

rime

rimed rim

Snowflakes are frequently decorated with small ice particles called rime. These are cloud droplets that collided with the crystals during flight and froze onto their surfaces. The droplets tend to be fairly uniform in size, with diameters around 0.03 mm (0.001 inches), which is about half the width of a human hair.

If you go snowflake watching with any regularity, you will soon witness the whole spectrum of rime coverage. Many snowfalls deliver crystals with a light dusting of rime particles. Usually the droplets are randomly scattered across the crystal faces, but aerodynamic forces may conspire to yield a crusty, rimed rim.

On some occasions, the flakes are plastered with such thick coatings that you can hardly make out their original forms, as in the example below. In the latter extreme, the precipitation is called *graupel*, or soft hail.

graupel

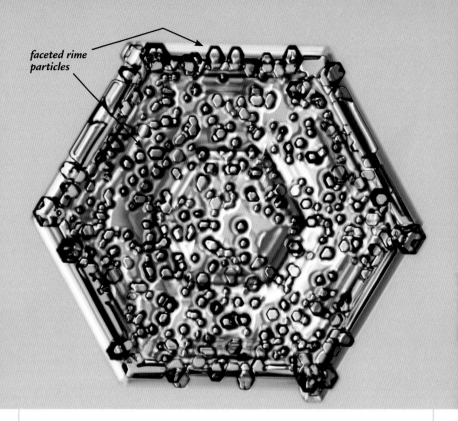

faceted rime particles

Case Study 7: Oriented Freezing. If you look carefully at the small snow crystal plate above, you can see that many of the rime particles are slightly faceted. These started out as cloud droplets made of liquid water, and they kept their round forms when they first froze on the surface. After some additional crystal growth, the solid droplets became faceted. If you study the photograph further, you can see that many of the small rime facets are aligned with respect to the larger facets of the main crystal.

This snow crystal plate illustrates a type of oriented freezing in which liquid droplets landing on an ice surface freeze with their molecular lattices matching the pre-existing lattice underneath. Thus, the water molecules in the main crystal and the frozen droplets are all aligned, making the composite structure a single ice crystal.

This phenomenon provides a ready explanation for some bizarrely shaped, asymmetrical snow crystals. Sometimes one or two rime droplets will strike a crystal and nucleate misplaced branches. These can subsequently develop into large, errant features that are otherwise hard to comprehend.

Snowflake Classification

Naming the different types of snowflakes presents a problem all its own. On one hand, there are obviously many distinct varieties out there. If you want to talk about them and understand them, then you have to start giving them names. A sensible nomenclature is a necessary first step.

On the other hand, snow crystal classification is necessarily ambiguous. There is no precise way to draw boundaries between the different types. Also, no matter how many distinct categories you define, you can always find crystals that do not belong in any of them.

There is some analogy with dogs. While there are many different canine breeds to choose from, exactly what you call a breed is a matter of debate, to be decided by committee. And no number of breeds is sufficient to include all individuals. Of course, snowflakes are much different than dogs, but trying to name them causes similar difficulties.

In this book, I organized snowflakes largely according to their growth behavior, and my choices for categories are shown on the facing page. I used the dominant growth mechanisms, described in the preceding pages, to provide a natural foundation for understanding the diversity of forms. These different crystal types, along with their causes and variations, are described in detail in Part II.

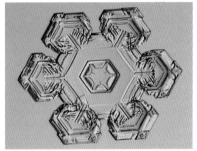

When snowflake watching, there is often no good answer to the question "What kind of snowflake is that?" Many snowflakes simply do not fit into any particular category. A more enlightened approach is to ask, "How did that snowflake grow into that shape?" No matter how unusual a specimen you find, the latter question must always have an answer.

Simple Prisms	Solid Columns	Sheaths	Scrolls on Plates	Triangular Forms
Hexagonal Plates	Hollow Columns	Cups	Columns on Plates	12-branched Stars
Stellar Plates	Bullet Rosettes	Capped Columns	Split Plates & Stars	Radiating Plates
Sectored Plates	Isolated Bullets	Multiply Capped Columns	Skeletal Forms	Radiating Dendrites
Simple Stars	Simple Needles	Capped Bullets	Twin Columns	Irregulars
Stellar Dendrites	Needle Clusters	Double Plates	Arrowhead Twins	Rimed
Fernlike Stellar Dendrites	Crossed Needles	Hollow Plates	Crossed Plates	Graupel

Types of Snow Crystals

The Origin of Snow

As a final stop before examining the different types of snowflakes, it is useful to look at how clouds form and how they go on to create snow. The story usually begins when the wind pushes a mass of warm, moist air into a different mass of air. This occurs frequently; what meteorologists call a weather front is simply the interface between two colliding air masses. Precipitation, including snowfall, often happens along such weather fronts.

If the collision pushes the warm air mass upward, then it cools as it rises. Once the air cools sufficiently, some of the water vapor it carries will condense into countless water droplets. Each droplet requires a nucleus on which to condense, and these are provided by particles of dust in the air. In aggregate, these liquid droplets are what you see as clouds.

If the newly formed clouds continue to cool, dust plays another role in making snow. Water droplets do not freeze immediately when the temperature is below 0° C (32° F); instead, they remain liquid in a supercooled state. Pure water droplets can be supercooled to nearly –40° C (–40° F) before they freeze. Dust provides a solid surface to jump-start the freezing process, so dusty droplets begin to freeze at around –6° C (21° F).

Once a droplet freezes into a miniature snowflake, it begins to grow and develop as water vapor condenses on its surface. The droplets that remain unfrozen slowly evaporate, supplying the air with water vapor for their frozen brethren. Thus, there is a net transfer of water molecules from liquid droplets to water vapor to snow crystals.

In a matter of minutes, depending on the snowfall, the frozen droplets will grow into full-sized snowflakes and drop out of the clouds. And, at the center of many snowflakes, too tiny for even the microscope to see, lies a solitary speck of dust that gave the crystal its start.

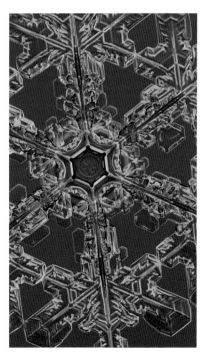

Part II

FIELD GUIDE

Hieroglyphics in Ice

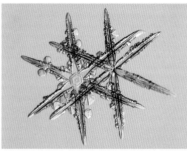

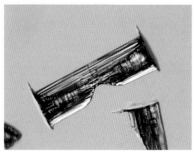

A snowflake is like a hieroglyph from the sky—the form and design of an individual crystal tell a story of its travels through the clouds. By examining a snowflake, you can learn about the conditions it experienced as it developed. Part of the fun of snowflake watching is trying to figure out how the different crystals grew into their various final shapes.

Bird watching, although similar in spirit to snowflake watching, does not afford this particular pleasure, nor does looking at plants or other living things. Life's biochemical machinery is almost unfathomable in its complexity, so extracting even a remotely fundamental understanding of anything alive is a Herculean task. But a snowflake is simple enough that one can actually comprehend quite a lot about how each crystal formed.

As I describe the different snow crystal types, I will endeavor to explain how each is formed. To this end, I will use the concepts and growth rules from Part I of this book to decipher how the various design features are created in the clouds.

The experience of watching snowflakes is greatly enhanced when you try to read the hieroglyphics. The more you understand about how the crystals develop and grow, the more fascinating these beautiful structures become.

Simple Prisms

Simple prisms are small, faceted snow crystals that can be either plate-like or columnar in form. They have relatively plain shapes, with minor patterning and no branching. These minimalist snowflakes are common and can be found during most snowfalls, regardless of temperature. However, most simple prisms are so tiny that you can only view them using a microscope.

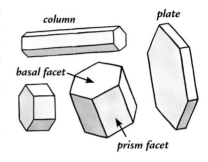

column   plate

basal facet

prism facet

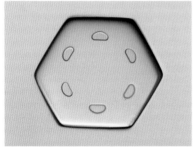

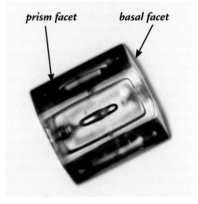

prism facet   basal facet

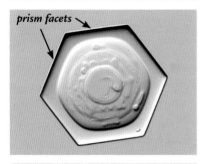

prism facets

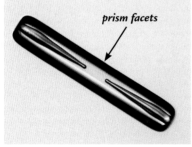

prism facets

Every snowflake has its beginning, and these small crystals are essentially young snowflakes that have not had time to grow into larger, more elaborate shapes. The examples shown here are roughly 0.3 mm (0.012 inches) in size, about as large as the period at the end of this sentence. Simple prisms are also called *diamond dust* crystals because they are small and faceted, like miniature ice jewels. However, the facets you see on gemstones are artificial, since they were put on with a grindstone, while snow crystal facets arise and grow spontaneously.

Faceting is the dominant force in the development of simple prisms because they are small. The transition to branching has not yet had a chance to occur. A rough rule of thumb is that branching begins when a crystal grows to more than half a millimeter (0.02 inches) in size, although this rule is only approximate. If the humidity is especially high, branching can occur sooner. If the humidity is low, crystals will remain faceted longer.

corners rounded by sublimation

Well-formed crystal facets have razor-sharp corners during growth, but this isn't always what you find in the pictures. Sublimation will often round the edges, as you can see with the small prism above. The erosion of sharp features is especially common on smaller specimens, and when the temperature is warm.

Sublimation is always an unknown factor when snowflake watching, since you don't know what conditions the different flakes have been through after forming. By the time it reaches the ground, a crystal may look quite different than it did when it was growing in the clouds.

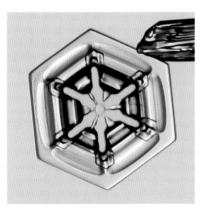

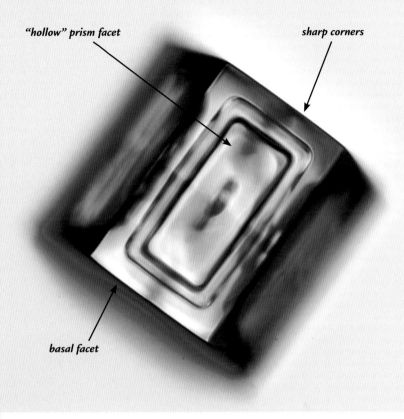

"hollow" prism facet

sharp corners

basal facet

Case Study 8: Hollow Facets. For this photograph, I focused my camera on one face of a diamond-dust prism, about 0.3 mm (0.012 inches) in size. I caught this crystal quickly on an especially cold day, so sublimation had not yet taken its toll; the corners are still distinct and sharp.

I like this picture because it's a good example of the hollowing sometimes seen in prism facets. During growth, diffusion gives the corners of the crystal a greater supply of water vapor. The facet centers receive less, so they accumulate material more slowly. With time, the facet centers lag behind the growth of the edges, as shown in the sketch at right. This is a common growth behavior and is the first step in the transition to branching (see page 19). Had this crystal grown larger, it soon would have abandoned its simple prism shape as it developed into a more complex structure.

Case Study 9: A Simple Hexagonal Plate. Crystals like this one are easy to find in most snowfalls, provided you use a microscope. All you usually have to do is let some snow fall onto a few glass slides, and then scan around looking for interesting specimens. Many of the snowflakes I've photographed were found using this straightforward technique.

The markings you see on this crystal were caused by variations in temperature and humidity it experienced during its travels. Each time its local environment changed, the crystal growth behavior changed. The resulting surface markings are mostly remnants of these variations in growth. Had the crystal formed under perfectly constant conditions, it would have ended up with smoother, mostly featureless basal surfaces.

Stellar Plates

S tellar plates are thin, flat crystals of medium size, with an overall sixfold symmetry. They are typically broad-branched, with little sidebranching and a profusion of complex surface markings. Stellar plates can be abundant when conditions are right. The best specimens are found during light snowfalls at fairly low temperatures.

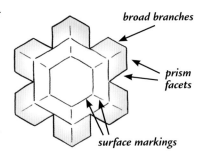

broad branches

prism facets

surface markings

The sparkle you see in falling snow often comes from stellar plates, when their flat basal surfaces catch the light. These crystals are large enough that a simple magnifier gives you a pretty good view of their overall structure. A good-sized specimen might be 2 mm (0.08 inches) in diameter, roughly the size of this "O." A microscope opens up yet another realm of observing, allowing you a detailed look at the intricate patterning on each crystal.

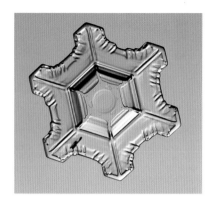

Stellar plates do not form at all temperatures, so they are not present during all snowfalls. The morphology diagram shows us that large, plate-like crystals will grow when the clouds are near either –15° C (5° F) or –2° C (28° F). At the higher temperature, one does not usually find well-formed crystals because of sublimation and other factors. The most stunning stellar crystals appear when the temperature is within a few degrees of –15° C (5° F). If you want to find beautiful stellar plates, you have to wait for just the right conditions.

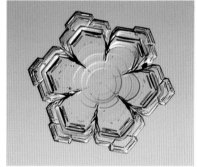

ribs

ridges

Case Study 10: Surface Patterns in Stellar Plates. One thing you quickly find
when watching snowflakes is that there is no such thing as an ordinary
stellar plate. Even when the outline of a crystal is relatively simple, as
with the above example, its surface patterns can be wonderfully rich and
complex. The abundance of surface markings is one of the main reasons
the character of each snowflake is so different from all the others.

Stellar plates have particularly elaborate patterns because their
growth is especially sensitive to humidity and temperature. They grow in
conditions where the branching instability and the knife-edge instability
are both near their respective thresholds. Thus, even minor changes in
the local environment affect the dynamics of these instabilities, which
in turn alters the growth behavior. Changes in growth leave behind various
sorts of remnant ridges and ribs, a bit like the crystalline equivalent of
tree rings (see page 24). Most of the markings you see above came about
when these basic features were generated over and over in a complex
series of temperature and humidity fluctuations.

Case Study 11: A Regal Snowflake. I found this rather majestic stellar crystal in Burlington, Vermont, while working a late-night snowfall from the cold rooftop of my hotel parking structure. Not an idyllic location, perhaps, but snowflakes are indifferent to where they fall. Be it a serene, snow-covered meadow or a midtown rooftop, the crystals fall about the same. I like parking structures when photographing at night because they are convenient and well lit.

This crystal measures just over 3 mm (0.12 inches) from tip to tip, which is on the large side for such a well-formed, lavishly decorated crystal.

Case Study 12: Rimed Regal. This snowflake is another product of Vermont, from the same snowfall as in the previous example. The two are similar in size, and both have broad, plate-like branches. The details are quite different because the crystals followed separate paths as they grew. This one caught some rime droplets near the end of its journey, which stuck to its outer parts and grew into small plates in random directions. Rime is often associated with large crystals, since the high humidity necessary for their growth is caused by a high density of cloud droplets.

Stellar plates are endlessly fascinating to observe. Not only are no two alike, but it's unusual to find two that are even similar. These crystals were all produced by a single snowfall in Michigan's Upper Peninsula.

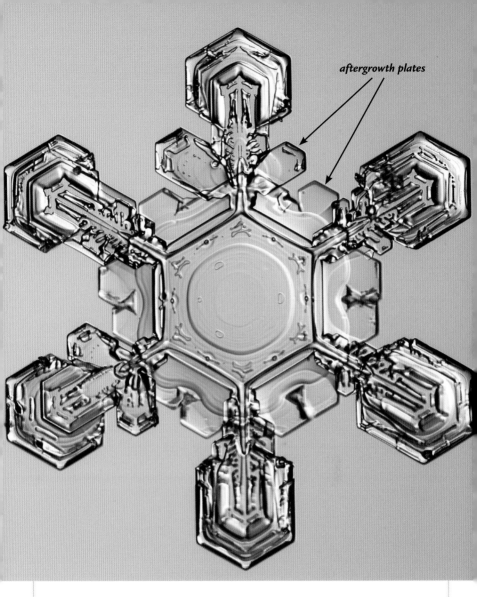

aftergrowth plates

Case Study 13: Aftergrowth Plates. Snowflakes mostly grow at their outer edges, which have the greatest supply of water vapor, but sometimes there is a crystal *aftergrowth* that fills in the inner regions. This growth occurs after a crystal has become quite large, and it tends to produce thin, rather featureless plates that are asymmetrically placed. Aftergrowth plates are especially likely if a crystal starts growing in low humidity, so the inner regions initially have substantial open spaces.

Case Study 14: Exotic Colors. Because snowflakes are made of ice, they are intrinsically transparent and colorless (see page 8). When I'm feeling especially creative, I like to experiment with different types of colored lighting. For the above photograph, I used a dark blue background augmented with various colored lights shining in from the sides. Where the crystal is thin and flat, like the inner regions of the main arms, you mostly see just the background coming through. But areas with more structure refract the other colors into the camera, yielding some flamboyant highlights.

Case Study 15: Rimed Stellar Plates. Many fine snowflakes have had their original identities obliterated by thick coatings of rime. This crystal first developed into a broad-branched stellar plate, probably with lots of surface patterning. The overall outline of the crystal, complete with regular facets on the branches, indicates that its initial growth was relatively undisturbed and free of rime. Then it encountered a dense fog and became coated with rime droplets.

Heavily rimed crystals like this one are especially common in warm, wet snowfalls. I took this picture in the Sierra Nevada Mountains of California, when the ground temperature was just below freezing. Nearly all the falling crystals that day had heavy coats of rime.

Some regions in the California mountains receive a lot of snow, so much that they even hold a few North American snowfall records. But quantity does not equal quality when it comes to snowflakes. In my travels, I've often found that regions with a lot of snowfall do not produce the most attractive snow crystals. Cold places with frequent, light snowfalls are usually better.

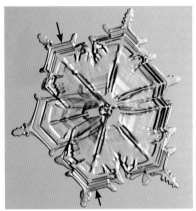

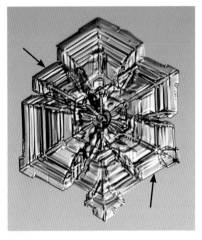

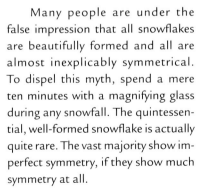

Many people are under the false impression that all snowflakes are beautifully formed and all are almost inexplicably symmetrical. To dispel this myth, spend a mere ten minutes with a magnifying glass during any snowfall. The quintessential, well-formed snowflake is actually quite rare. The vast majority show imperfect symmetry, if they show much symmetry at all.

The above pictures provide several examples of malformed stellar plates. These are all single crystals of ice, as you can see from the way the prism facets on each are aligned relative to one another. Notice, for instance, how the facets on opposite sides run parallel, as indicated by arrows in the photographs. The facets reveal the underlying molecular order, which is the same throughout each plate.

The odd shapes of these crystals came about because their growth was disturbed in some way. Perhaps they experienced some lattice defects during growth, or they collided with rime particles or other falling crystals. There are many potential problems that can interfere with symmetrical growth.

Sectored Plates

S ectored plates are flat, broad-branched crystals decorated with a pronounced radiating pattern of symmetrical ridges. Their name comes from the way the ridges seem to neatly divide the plates into sectors. At times, these surface markings look like veins on a leaf, giving some snowflakes an almost plantlike appearance.

Sectored plates are a subclass of stellar plates; they grow best when cloud temperatures are near that magic value of –15° C (5° F), although respectable specimens can also be found at around –2° C (28° F).

The relative simplicity of their surface markings indicates that sectored plates form in relatively constant conditions, without large swings in temperature or humidity. Thus the plate-like branches are generally flat and smooth (aside from the ridges), and the prism facets tend to be well-formed and large.

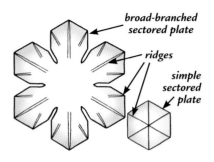

broad-branched sectored plate

ridges

simple sectored plate

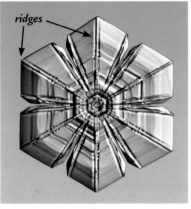

ridges

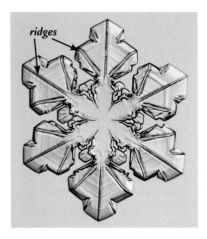

ridges

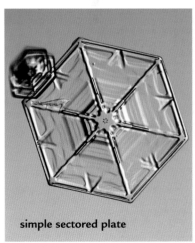

simple sectored plate

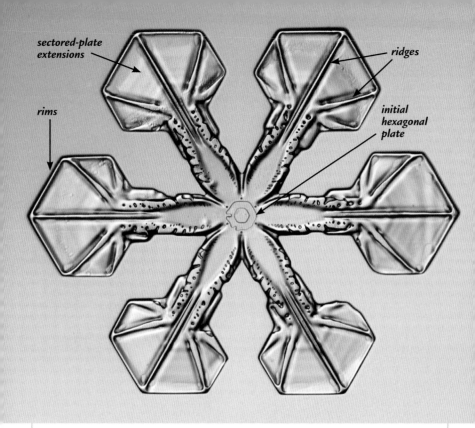

sectored-plate extensions

ridges

rims

initial hexagonal plate

Case Study 16: Sectored Plate Extensions. Occasionally, the broad branches of a stellar crystal will be subdivided by ridges, as in the above example. A descriptive name for this specimen might be a "broad-branched stellar crystal with sectored-plate extensions."

You can get a pretty good picture of how this crystal formed by examining its features in detail. It started out as a tiny hexagonal plate, and you can still see an imperfect outline of this initial form in the photograph. As the crystal grew, the branching instability soon produced six symmetrical branches, which then grew into twigs without significant sidebranching.

After the branches grew out a while, the temperature and humidity changed to favor plate-like growth, which resulted in the formation of large, thin plates at the ends of the arms. As the plates grew out, ridges divided them into sectors. Near the end of its growth, the edges thickened and rims appeared around each plate. Finally, the crystal happened to fall onto my collection board, where I picked it up and captured its image. The entire process, from birth to photograph, took about fifteen minutes.

You can find ridges in many types of snow crystals, but they are especially prominent in broad-branched stellar plates.

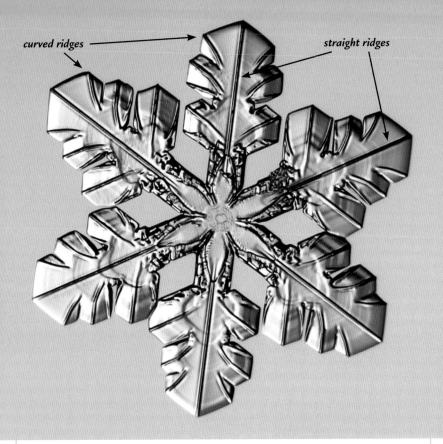

curved ridges

straight ridges

Case Study 17: Curved Ridges. In the above crystal, you can see how each of the many ridges is associated with a corner between two prism facets. If the facets on both sides of a ridge grow at the same rate, then the ridge will grow out straight. If the growth rates change with time, the ridge may become curved.

The diagram at right shows the outline of a branch at four different times during its growth. At first, the side facets grew slowly, but later they picked up speed. As a result of this changing growth, the side ridges became curved.

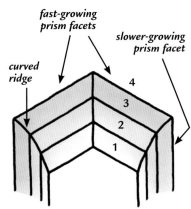

fast-growing prism facets

slower-growing prism facet

curved ridge

1 2 3 4

Growth of a Sectored Branch*. Numbers show the branch outline at different times. Note how the ridges trace where the corners were as the crystal grew.*

sectored-plate branches

first sectored plate

double grooves

Case Study 18: Sectored Branches. The sharply faceted snowflake above underwent a double episode of sectored branching. When it was about half its final size, the crystal looked essentially like the example at right—a classic sectored plate. But then something happened— probably a brief rise in humidity—that stimulated the growth of a new set of sectored plate branches, extending from the first.

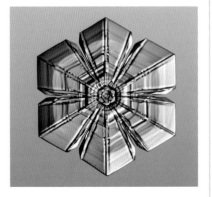

Stellar Dendrites

S tellar dendrites are plate-like crystals with narrow branches decorated with numerous sidebranches. They are larger than stellar plates and generally have less prominent faceting and more complex shapes. These crystals can be readily found with the naked eye, and considerable detail can be seen with a simple magnifier. Stellar dendrites are common in many snowfalls, often arriving in great numbers.

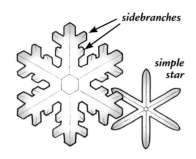

The word dendrite means "tree-like," which is an apt description of these extravagant crystals. The largest ones appear around –15° C (5° F) when the humidity is high. The ample water-vapor supply vigorously drives the branching instability to produce numerous sidebranches.

Stellar dendrites are always conspicuous, since a generously sized specimen might be 3 mm (0.12 inches) from tip to tip, and larger ones can be found. They are frequently thin and lacy in appearance.

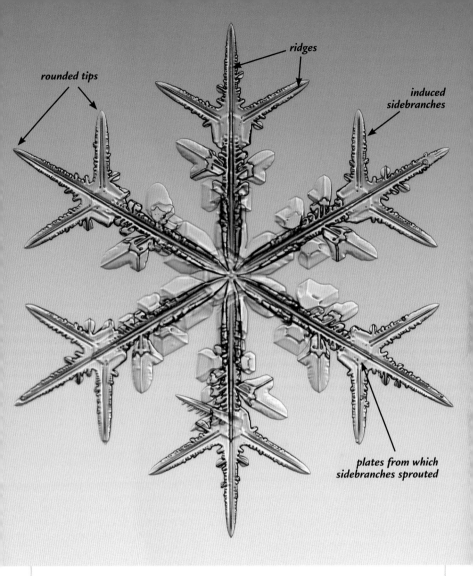

rounded tips

ridges

induced
sidebranches

plates from which
sidebranches sprouted

Case Study 19: A Classic Stellar Dendrite. This crystal shows many of the standard features of stellar dendrites. Note how the branch tips are rounded, which is an indication that the growth was too fast to form prism facets. Note also the distinct ridges centered on each branch like spines. These are both common sights in thin-branched crystals. This particular specimen also shows a major induced sidebranching event. If you look closely, you can see outlines of the small, faceted plates from which the sidebranches sprouted.

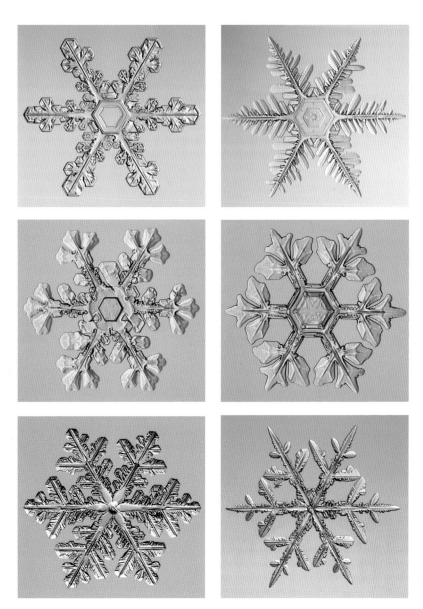

The growth of stellar dendrites, like stellar plates, is sensitive to temperature and humidity, resulting in a broad diversity of forms. Stellar-dendrite branches can have any number of sidebranches, with different degrees of faceting.

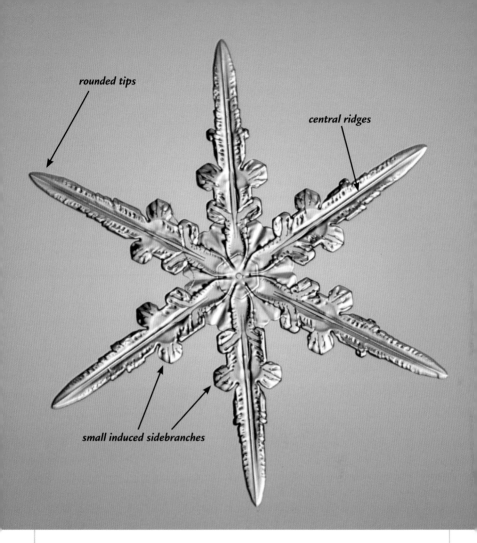

rounded tips

central ridges

small induced sidebranches

Case Study 20: Simple Stars.
Sometimes the humidity is high enough that a snow crystal sprouts branches, but not high enough to produce much sidebranching. This results in simple stellar crystals like these, where the arms are little more than featureless, straight twigs. Both these crystals are just under 2 mm (0.08 inches) in size.

ridges

backward branches

Case Study 21: Backward Branching. On rare occasions, you can find a snow crystal with some branches growing backward, as shown above. This is in contrast to the majority of cases where the branches grow outward, toward the source of water vapor. Regardless of direction, ridged branches are all separated from one another by multiples of 60 degrees. The sidebranches in stellar dendrites generally grow parallel to neighboring branches.

Fernlike Stellar Dendrites

Fernlike stellar dendrites are large, thin plates with narrow branches and sidebranches, and overall the crystals look like tiny ferns. The sidebranches are all oriented at 60-degree angles with respect to one another, running parallel to neighboring branches. These crystals are common, and their exceptionally large size makes them easy to spot.

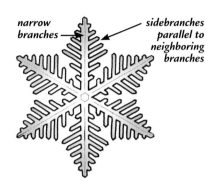

narrow branches — sidebranches parallel to neighboring branches

Fernlike stellar dendrites are the largest snowflakes, on rare occasions measuring over 10 mm (0.4 inches) in size. Their thickness may be a hundred times less than this, however, making them extremely thin, flat, plate-like crystals. They mostly form near –15° C (5° F) when the humidity is especially high. Their rapid growth drives the formation of copious sidebranches.

The well-defined angles between the branches and sidebranches of fernlike stellar dendrites indicate that they are single crystals of ice. In spite of their complex shapes, the molecules are all lined up from one tip to the other.

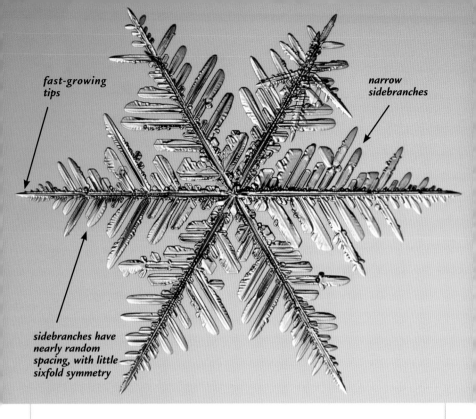

fast-growing tips

narrow sidebranches

sidebranches have nearly random spacing, with little sixfold symmetry

Case Study 22: Branching Run Amok. The shape of this snow crystal reflects the humid environment in which it grew. As soon as it was born, the abundance of water vapor drove the branching instability hard, so the transition from faceted to branched growth occurred early. As a result, there is no visible remnant of the crystal's initial faceted stage at its center.

Once the principal arms were established, the high humidity resulted in narrow, closely spaced sidebranches with little prism faceting. The absence of faceting meant no induced sidebranching events, and thus no sixfold symmetry in the placement of the sidebranches. In a sense, the growth of this crystal was too fast to be orchestrated.

This is a medium-sized dendritic specimen, just over 2 mm (0.08 inches) from tip to tip, but it is also quite thin and flat. Basal faceting, with some assistance from the knife-edge instability, mainly restricted its growth to two dimensions. Since it stayed thin and light, it made a slow descent through the clouds, typically falling no faster than 1 mile per hour. Fernlike stellar dendrites fall more slowly than other snow crystals, giving them more time to grow.

induced
sidebranching

aftergrowth
plates

hexagonal
remnant

Case Study 23: In-depth Analysis. This colorful *objet d'art* tells a good story of how it formed. The crystal began its life as a small hexagonal plate that quickly sprouted six principal arms. The humidity wasn't as high as in the previous example, so you can still see a hexagonal remnant near the center. At first the arms grew lean, like straight twigs with little sidebranching, indicating a moderate humidity.

When the arms were at about 40 percent of their final length, the humidity must have dropped further, so that small faceted plates grew at the arm tips. Then the crystal fell into a denser region of the clouds, which made the humidity rise again, producing a strong induced sidebranching event. From then on, the arms grew out rapidly with lots of sidebranching until the crystal reached its final size of 2.4 mm (0.1 inches). The sidebranches are somewhat broader and not so closely spaced as in the previous example, which again indicates a lower humidity. But the crystal is larger, so it therefore spent a bit more time in the clouds.

While the outer arms were growing, the inner regions experienced higher humidity. The lack of earlier sidebranching meant these areas were still rather open, and so they filled in with aftergrowth plates.

Case Study 24: A Monster Snowflake. I've been watching snowflakes long enough to observe some really huge fernlike stellar dendrites. The one above measured 10.2 mm (0.4 inches) from tip to tip, about as large as a dime. I've only seen monster crystals like this in northern Ontario, a region that seems to specialize in really big snowflakes. It's quite a sight to see such enormous ice flowers drifting through the air and landing on your sleeve! Even at my microscope's lowest magnification, I had to capture this specimen in four separate photographs, which I later stitched together on my computer.

This crystal exhibits some fractal, or self-similar, structure. Many sidebranches have their own sidebranches, and some of them even have additional sidebranches.

Case Study 25: Interlocking Crystals. When conditions are right for the formation of dendritic crystals, they can fall in abundance. This picture shows a close-up view of the windshield of my car after a snowfall that dropped large stellar snowflakes almost exclusively. You can see how the barbed branches locked together to form an exceptionally light, fluffy blanket of ice. Any sound that strikes such a structure is efficiently absorbed by friction between the crystals. After this snowfall, the world was a very quiet place.

Hollow Columns

Hollow columns are simple hexagonal ice prisms with conical voids extending down from their ends. The recesses typically come in a symmetric pair running along the central axis of a crystal, with the tips nearly touching at the waist. Hollow columns are difficult to see with the naked eye, and their internal structure is best viewed with a microscope. They are a common columnar morphology and can frequently be found during warmer snowfalls.

Hollow columns usually form when the temperature is near –5° C (23° F), as noted in the morphology diagram. Their hexagonal structure is often not apparent because the corners have been eroded by sublimation, which is especially rapid at warmer temperatures. Thus, hollow columns tend to look like round cylinders.

The crystals pictured here are fairly small, close to a millimeter (0.04 inches) in length; the one at right is slightly shorter, the one below is longer. They're small enough that you might call them diamond dust, but that term is usually reserved for crystals with more distinct facets.

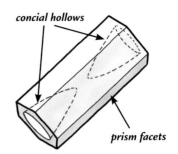

concial hollows

prism facets

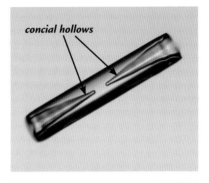

concial hollows

Hollow columns can also grow below –20° C (–4° F), but snowfalls are rare at such low temperatures. When air cools down, the water vapor it carries usually participates out before it gets that cold. Then the air becomes dry, and people say, "It's too cold to snow." (It would be more accurate to say, "It's too dry to snow.")

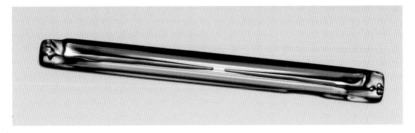

The formation of a hollow column is another manifestation of the familiar branching instability. The diagram at right shows cross-sections of a hollow column at different times during its growth. When the crystal was small, faceting was the dominant growth mechanism, and it quickly became a solid column. As the crystal grew larger, diffusion began to limit its growth. The corners stuck out farther, and thus began to grow faster. Soon, the basal facets became concave and the instability accelerated. After a while, the recesses were so shielded that they ceased growing altogether.

You can see how this picture nicely shows the various features of hollow columns. For example, the two hollow regions never actually touch at the center of a crystal because the structure always starts out as a solid prism, with the hollows forming as the crystal grows. All snow crystals have solid centers for this reason.

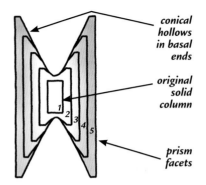

conical hollows in basal ends

original solid column

prism facets

Growth of a hollow column (shown in cross section). *Numbers show the crystal at different times. Note how the corners of the crystal grew out to leave the voids behind.*

We can also explain the conical shape of the voids by looking at the growth profiles shown in the diagram. During growth, the diameter of the end of the void is nearly as large as the total diameter of the column. Both diameters increase as the column grows longer, so the hollows end up with a conical shape.

Finally, we note that the bipolar symmetry of hollow columns has the same basic origin as the sixfold symmetry of stellar plates. The two ends of a column experience the same conditions at the same times, so naturally they grow in synchrony. It all begins to make sense once you know the basic rules of snow crystal growth.

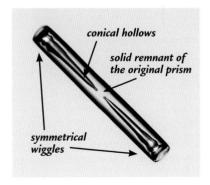

conical hollows

solid remnant of the original prism

symmetrical wiggles

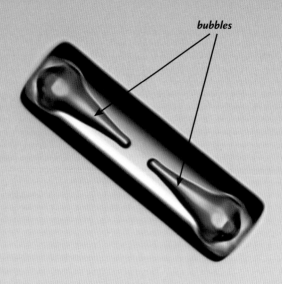

bubbles

Case Study 26: Bubbles in Ice. Not every hollow column follows the standard growth plan. Each crystal takes a different path through the clouds, so interesting things can happen. Sometimes the ends of a hollow column will grow in such a way that the outer surface of the crystal becomes that of a solid prism again. When that happens, it leaves behind a symmetrical pair of bubbles trapped inside the ice.

bubbles

This growth behavior may result when a hollow column experiences a sudden drop in temperature and humidity. The lower temperature will favor the formation of plates rather than columns, and the lower humidity will favor faceting over branching. Together these effects can fill in the holes in the basal facets, covering the recesses in the process. Bubbles often go unnoticed because of their small size, but they are present in quite a few snow crystals.

Needles

Needles are especially long, slender columnar crystals. The simplest examples are essentially extra-tall hollow columns, but usually they develop more complex shapes. Needles are easy to spot with the naked eye, looking like short bits of white hair on your sleeve. Their detailed structures are best viewed with the aid of a microscope or a strong magnifier. Needles are common, and they sometimes appear in great numbers.

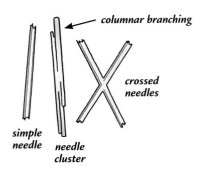

columnar branching

crossed needles

simple needle

needle cluster

Needle crystals are the products of warm, wet snowfalls, forming when the temperature is close to –5° C (23° F) and the humidity is high. With lengths up to 3 mm (0.12 inches), needles are the longest of the columnar snow crystals.

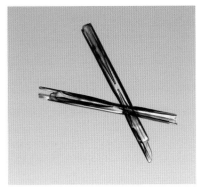

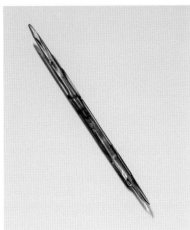

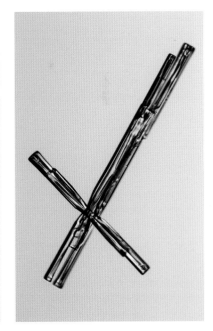

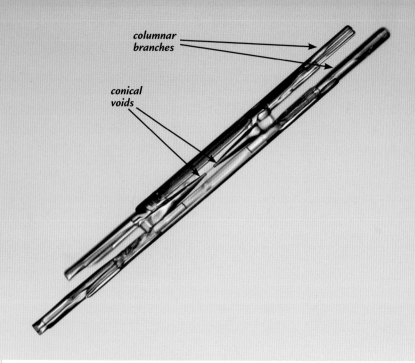

columnar branches

conical voids

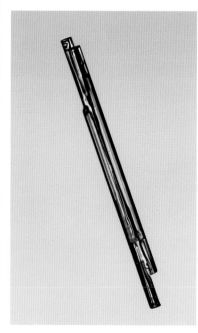

Case Study 27: Split Ends. Linear clusters of needles form when the ends of a single column split into several distinct needles. Consider, for example, the formation of the above specimen. You can see conical voids inside the crystal, showing that it started as a simple hollow column. Since the initial column was hexagonal, like a wooden pencil, each of its ends had six corners. The branching instability began working on these corners, and some soon sprouted branches. Because the growth of the crystal was columnar, the branches were themselves needle-shaped. Needle clusters are a common morphology, and they are all produced by variations on this basic theme.

Capped Columns

Capped columns are columnar crystals with stellar plates on their ends. A typical specimen looks like a stubby axle flanked by two hexagonal wheels. These crystals are relatively uncommon, but you can sometimes find a few mixed in with simple columnar crystals during warmer snowfalls. Capped columns are just large enough to be spotted with the naked eye, and their distinctive dumbbell shape makes them easy to identify.

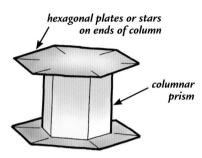

hexagonal plates or stars on ends of column

columnar prism

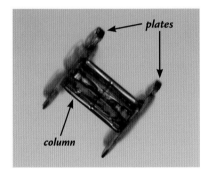

plates

column

Capped columns are also called *tsuzumi crystals*, named after a small hourglass-shaped Japanese drum.

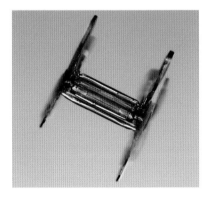

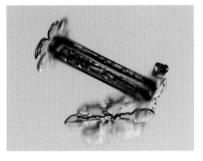

A capped column forms when a snow crystal experiences its own style of midlife crisis, suddenly changing its growth behavior from columnar to plate-like. This can happen when a large mass of air is pushed upward by a passing storm front. The air cools as it rises, carrying suspended cloud droplets along with it. When the temperature falls to around –6° C (21° F), some of the droplets freeze into nascent snowflakes. At this temperature, the crystals begin growing into columns. If the air continues to rise, and the temperature drops to around –15° C (5° F), additional growth will be plate-like, resulting in capped columns.

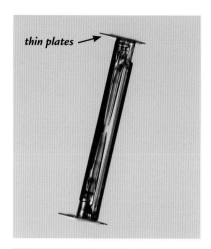

thin plates →

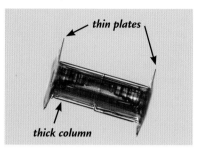

thin plates

thick column

A noteworthy feature of capped columns is that the transition from columnar axle to plate-like ends is almost always abrupt. A typical crystal looks as though two thin plates were glued onto the ends of an otherwise ordinary ice column, as in the two examples at the top of the page.

This appearance suggests that the growth transition was rapid—a simple column grew for a while and then, boom, suddenly thin plates started growing. Temperature changes are usually gradual, yet you almost never encounter a capped column with a gradual transition in shape.

The knife-edge instability is the solution to this puzzle, since abrupt behavior is the nature of an instability. When it begins, thin edges form on the ends of the column, as in the two pictures on the left.

Once a sharp edge forms, the instability accelerates the plate growth. If these two crystals had continued growing, they too would have developed large, thin end plates.

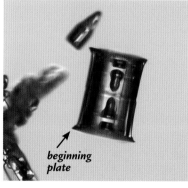

beginning
plate

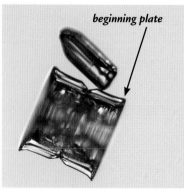

beginning plate

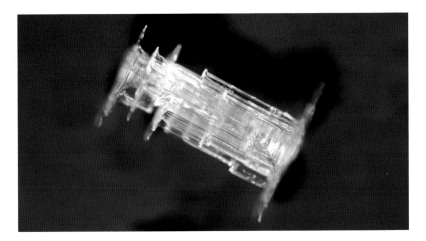

In addition to simple capped columns, you might also find some *multiply capped columns* like those shown here. These crystals have more than just two stellar plates on the column ends; they have additional plates, or perhaps partial plates, growing out from various ledges on the sides of their columns.

Multiply capped columns form when complex columnar clusters switch to plate-like growth. They're not particularly rare, in spite of their unusual appearance, because imperfectly formed columns are not rare.

A ledge or blemish of any kind on the side of a column may nucleate the growth of a plate. These can come from crystal growth defects or the type of branching that produces needle clusters. Sometimes a rime droplet will provide a nucleation site when it freezes onto the side of a column.

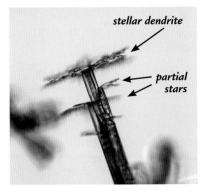

stellar dendrite

partial stars

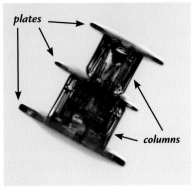

plates

columns

multiple plates (seen from side) growing from rime particles

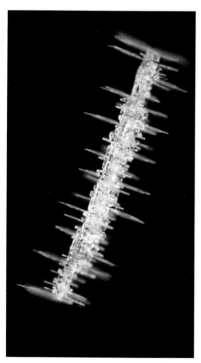

Case Study 28: Fuzzy Caterpillars. The world of multiply capped columns is inhabited by some exotic beasts, such as the two ice caterpillars shown on this page. Both are relatively simple needle crystals festooned with copious side plates. (The plates are all seen edge-on in the pictures.) Each of these crystals started out as a simple needle, which then became coated with rime. Next, the temperature dropped and plates sprouted from many of the rime droplets. Note that the rime froze with the same lattice orientation as the underlying needles (see page 29). The fact that the side plates are all parallel to one another reveals that each of these wooly creatures is a single crystal of ice. The water molecules are aligned throughout.

Case Study 29: Capped Column Close-up. The three photographs at right show the same crystal, but with two different orientations and with different focal planes.

The top picture shows the crystal as I found it, after it had fallen onto a glass slide. This shows a nice side view of the column upon which the plates formed. Some hollowing is present, so at one point this crystal must have looked like a simple hollow column.

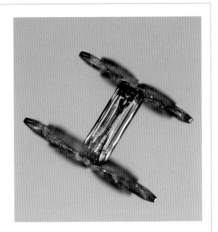

After taking the first photograph, I used a fine paintbrush to carefully flip the crystal over onto one of the stellar plate faces. Focusing my microscope on the smaller upper plate yielded the second picture, which looks like a pretty typical stellar plate. The symmetry is subtly imperfect, and you can see a dark spot where the column attaches.

Without moving the crystal, I then focused on the lower plate to produce the third picture. Note the blurry upper plate obscures its sibling to some degree. The lower plate looks a lot like the upper one, as you would expect, since the two formed under nearly identical conditions.

As they grew, the two plates inevitably began competing for water vapor. By chance one became slightly larger, so it started receiving more water vapor and it grew faster. Had this crystal continued to develop, the larger plate would eventually have dwarfed the smaller one.

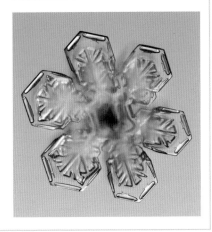

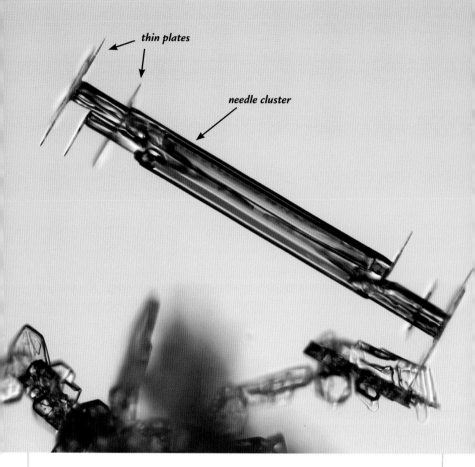

thin plates

needle cluster

Case Study 30: Capped Needles. The excellent specimen above is one of my favorite capped columns. It might be more appropriately called a capped needle, since plates are growing from the ends of a sizable needle cluster. The crystal is about 1.7 mm (0.07 inches) long.

A noteworthy feature of this crystal is that the end plates are all amazingly thin, with razor-sharp edges. In addition, the column-to-plate transitions are especially abrupt. This is an excellent demonstration of the knife-edge instability in action.

I've encountered large capped needles like this only once, on a remarkable day on Michigan's Upper Peninsula. Over a period of just half an hour, I spotted a fairly large number of extraordinary capped columns like this one. When the conditions are just right, rare snow crystals can fall in abundance.

Double Plates

Double plates are pairs of thin, plate-like crystals sandwiched together with stout columns connecting them. Often one side is a large stellar plate, while the other is a smaller hexagon, but many other variations are possible. This phenomenon is relatively common, and many stellar crystals are actually double plates.

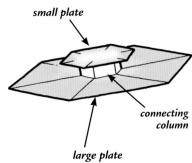

small plate

connecting column

large plate

plates

short column

plates

A double plate forms when a thick plate or stubby prism grows into two closely separated thin plates, as seen in the above examples (both seen edge-on). These crystals are basically extreme versions of capped columns, and the formation mechanism and temperatures are quite similar.

Since the two plates are so closely spaced, they compete fiercely for water vapor. If one becomes dominant, it soon overshadows the other and stunts its growth. The example at right shows two views of a rimed double plate, with the microscope focused separately on the two layers.

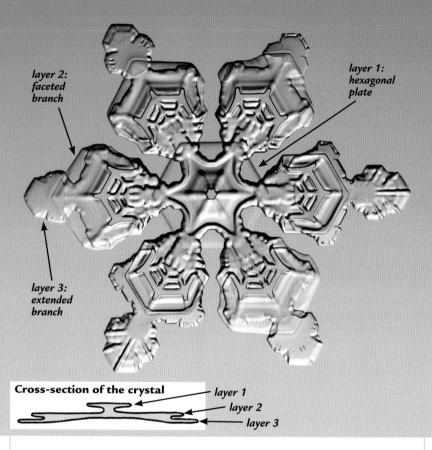

layer 2:
faceted
branch

layer 1:
hexagonal
plate

layer 3:
extended
branch

Cross-section of the crystal — layer 1

— layer 2

— layer 3

Case Study 31: A Multilayered Plate. This may look like an ordinary stellar crystal at first glance, but upon closer inspection you can make out three distinct layers, as shown in cross-section in the inset diagram.

First, note the nicely formed hexagonal plate near the center of the crystal (layer 1), which is slightly out of focus in this picture. This hexagon was one-half of a double plate when the crystal was small. The other half grew out faster and branched, depriving the hexagon of water vapor. Since it grew relatively slowly, the hexagon remained smaller and faceted. You often see double plates where the larger sheet is branched and the smaller one is faceted.

When the crystal was about half its final size, it ran into low humidity and the branches grew thicker. Later, the humidity picked up and the branches became double plates of their own (layers 2 and 3). Here again, one plate was left behind growing slowly (layer 2) while the other grew out more quickly (layer 3). Many stellar crystals are made from multiple layers like this one.

Hollow Plates

Hollow plates are thick plates with voids extending down from their prism faces. Sometimes the faces grow over the voids, enclosing thin bubbles in the ice. Hollows and bubbles are fairly common in many snow crystal types, but they are easily overlooked.

Hollow plates are essentially the plate-like equivalent of hollow columns (see page 64). A hollow plate starts out as a faceted, thick-plate crystal. As it grows, the facet edges tend to grow faster than the centers. With time, this can leave voids in the prism faces, as shown in the diagram.

Hollow plates are most likely to grow when the temperature is between where columns and thin plates form, so around –12° C (10° F). Thick plates form at this temperature, and they become hollow if the humidity is right. Fluctuations in temperature and humidity sometimes give the voids rather odd shapes, as in the crystal at the upper right. More often the voids are wide and fairly shallow, as seen in the hollow branch below.

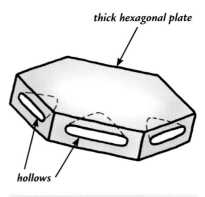

thick hexagonal plate

hollows

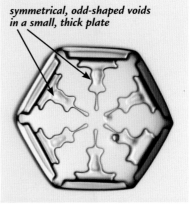

symmetrical, odd-shaped voids in a small, thick plate

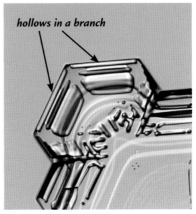

hollows in a branch

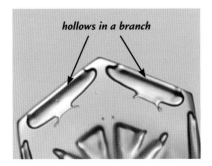

hollows in a branch

hollow-plate branches

out-of-focus hexegonal plate

Case Study 32: A Thick Stellar Plate. It may look a bit odd, but if you've been paying attention thus far, you should be able to recognize a number of unusual features in this snow crystal. The large blurry region in the center indicates that this specimen is a double-plate crystal. One plate is branched and in focus; the other is a smaller hexagonal plate that is considerably out of focus in this picture. Also, the tips of the branches are well-formed hollow plates with rather deep recesses in each of the outer prism facets. These features are all indicative of thick-plate crystals, which suggests that this specimen probably grew at a temperature around –12° C (10° F).

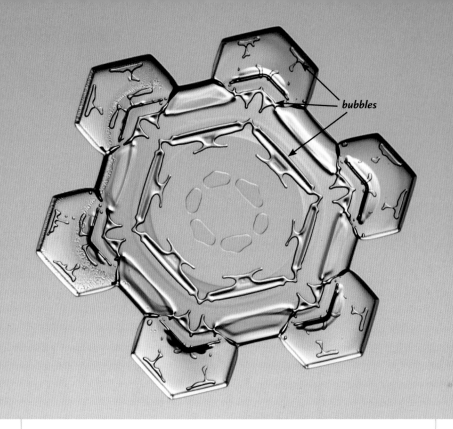

bubbles

Case Study 33: Bubbles in Plates.
Much of the internal structure in
the above crystal comes from bubbles in the ice. The close-up at right
shows some of these in more detail.

The bubbles formed when
hollows in the plate grew over to
enclose voids, which is the hollow-
plate analog of the process that
makes bubbles in hollow columns
(see page 64). It's not always easy
to tell internal voids from surface
structures, but bubbles usually
have rounded surfaces with rather
odd shapes. Snow crystals contain-
ing bubbles have a fluid look that I
find especially attractive.

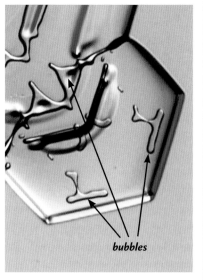

bubbles

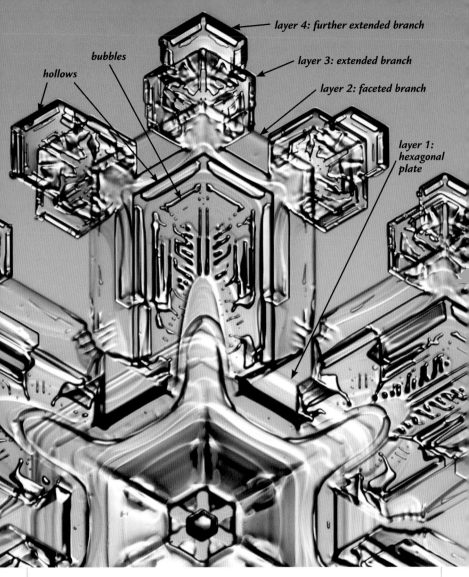

layer 4: further extended branch

bubbles

hollows

layer 3: extended branch

layer 2: faceted branch

layer 1: hexagonal plate

Case Study 34: Double Plates, Hollow Plates, and Bubbles. A close inspection of this crystal, shown in full on page 42, reveals a host of novel design elements. It forms an impressive quadruple-layered structure, and within the branches you can see various hollows and bubbles. This is also a thick-plate crystal that grew at temperatures around –12° C (10° F), similar to the previous examples. The multilayered structure with hollows and bubbles gives this crystal a particularly exotic look.

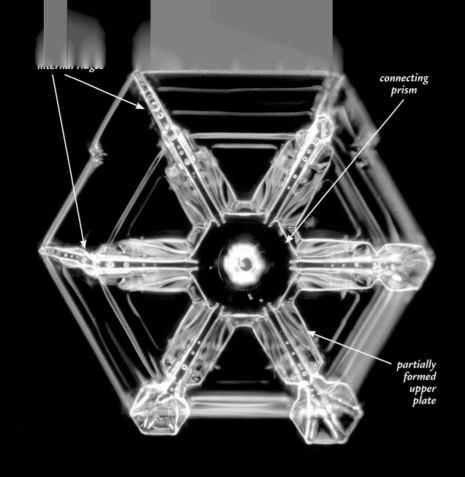

internal ridges

connecting
prism

partially
formed
upper
plate

Case Study 35: Skeletal Structure. This picture shows a close-up view of a small specimen, just 0.8 mm (0.03 inches) from tip to tip. The crystal started out as a small, blocky hexagonal prism. As it grew larger, the crystal developed a deep hollow-plate structure. Soon, one side of the hollow plate began to dominate the growth, robbing water vapor from the other side. The stunted side was then unable to grow into a complete plate. This is called *skeletal growth* because the structure is like a light framework of ice supported by internal ridges.

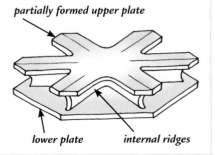

partially formed upper plate

lower plate   *internal ridges*

Split Plates and Split Stars

*S*plit crystals are double plates that have experienced asymmetrical growth. A typical example is when a portion of one plate becomes large, along with the opposite portion of the other plate. The end result consists of two partial plates joined at the center. These snowflakes are commonly mixed in with normal stellar plates, and they can be recognized by their split appearance. Sometimes you can find isolated partial plates after the two parts of a split crystal have separated during flight.

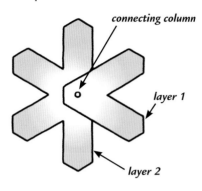

The formation of a split crystal is driven by a growth competition between the two members of a double plate. The plates start out symmetrical, but as soon as one edges ahead, it starves the other of water vapor and retards its growth. If one entire ice sheet dominates, the result is a double plate. But if parts of both plates prevail, then the crystal is a split plate. If the dominant parts are branched, the crystal is called a split star.

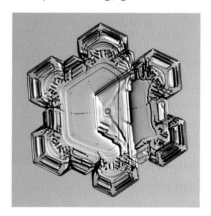

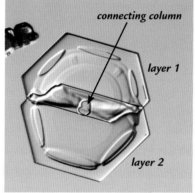

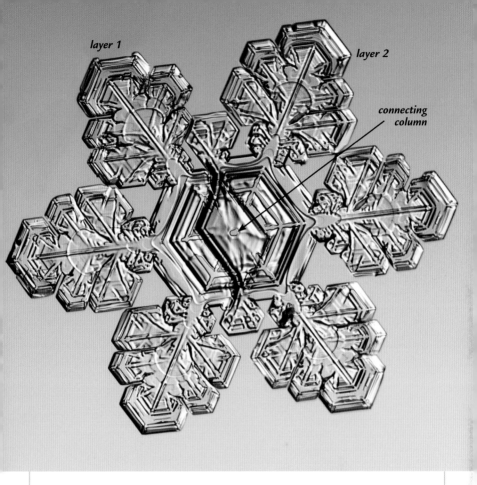

layer 1

layer 2

connecting column

Case Study 36: A Classic Split Star. Although this snow crystal has a rather odd shape, its growth history is easy to deduce. It started in the usual way, as a minute cloud droplet that froze and quickly grew into a tiny, hexagonal prism. In these first faceted minutes, the crystal was probably blocky in form, with roughly equal height and width.

After a bit of time passed, the conditions changed to favor the growth of thin plates. The knife-edge instability kicked in and soon the simple prism became a double plate. Briefly the two plates grew at the same rate, but soon the right half of one plate became dominant, as did the left half of the other. The assembly continued to grow as a faceted split plate until arms sprouted, at which point the six dominant arms grew fairly symmetrically, finally yielding the crystal you see above. It almost looks like a normal stellar plate, except that the two sets of arms do not quite point to a common center.

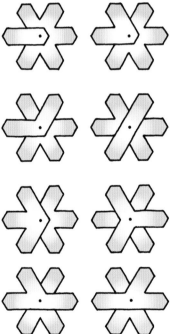

While split plates tend to form in roughly equal halves, split stars come in the eight different varieties shown at left. When the two sides of a double plate each sprout six arms, the result is essentially six separate growth races, with these eight possible outcomes of the races.

The crystal above is a 4+2 split star, the fourth type in the diagram. The fragment below was made when a crystal with the same geometry broke into pieces.

The eight ways to make a split star.

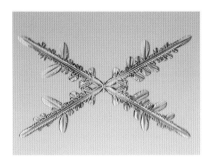

Scrolls and Chandeliers

Scrolls and columns appear on plates when the growth of a crystal changes from plate-like to columnar. Occasionally, a single crystal will go from columnar to plate-like to columnar again, yielding some especially exotic shapes. Examples are rare, and they are most often found during warmer snowfalls, mixed in with much greater numbers of ordinary crystals.

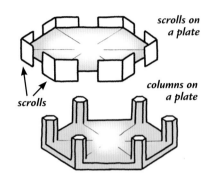

scrolls on a plate

columns on a plate

scrolls

The two forms in the diagram are analogous to capped columns, except that the growth switches from plate-like to columnar, rather than the other way around. Capped columns are much more common than either of these forms because of how storm fronts work (see page 69).

I like to call these *chandelier crystals* on account of their elaborate shapes. The two pictures on the right show crystals that first started out as thick columns, then became capped columns, and finally grew columns or scrolls on the outer edges of their plates. Such crystals are rare because they need to undergo an unusual series of temperature changes.

columns

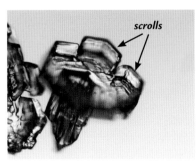

scrolls

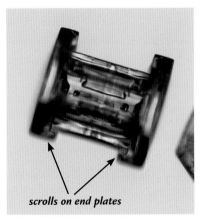

scrolls on end plates

Bullet Rosettes

A bullet rosette is a collection of columnar crystals that formed together around a single nucleus. Competition for water vapor inhibits growth near the center, giving each column a bulletlike shape. Isolated bullets come from the breakup of rosettes. These crystals are typically found mixed with columnar crystals during warmer snowfalls. Capped bullet rosettes appear with capped columns.

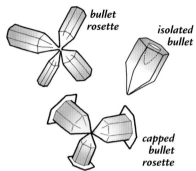

bullet
rosette

isolated
bullet

capped
bullet
rosette

Bullet rosette

competition
for water
vapor

prism facets

Bullet rosettes are polycrystalline forms, which means that the entire structure is made of several individual crystals joined together with random orientations. In contrast, all the snowflake types discussed so far have been single ice crystals.

A polycrystal typically forms when a liquid cloud droplet freezes quickly, forming defects in the ice lattice. Because the different crystal pieces are not precisely oriented, the overall structure is not symmetrical like a single crystal.

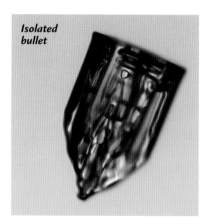

**Isolated
bullet**

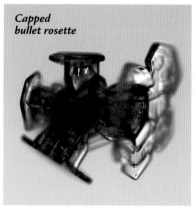

**Capped
bullet rosette**

Radiating Plates and Dendrites

R*adiating plates are polycrystalline forms much like bullet rosettes, except with a collection of plates instead of columns. Typically, the different segments grow out from a common center, and their structure can be anything from simple faceted plates to fernlike dendrites. These composite structures are common and are typically found mixed in with other plate-like crystals.*

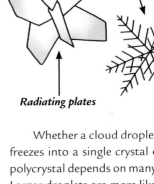

Radiating dendrites
(also called Spatial dendtrites)

Radiating plates

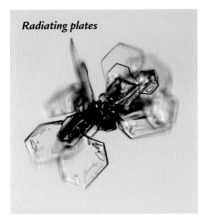

Radiating plates

Whether a cloud droplet initially freezes into a single crystal or into a polycrystal depends on many factors. Larger droplets are more likely to become polycrystalline, as are droplets with greater amounts of trapped dust.

Polycrystals can also form when particles collide and stick. The crystal below probably picked up a rime droplet that froze with some random crystal orientation. This nucleated the extra branches you see growing out of the plane of the photograph.

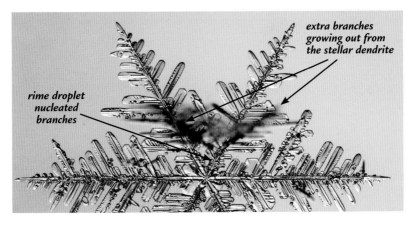

extra branches growing out from the stellar dendrite

rime droplet nucleated branches

Sheaths

*S*heaths are exaggerated hollow columns with exceptionally thin walls, a bit like slender wine glasses. Sheaths are rare, appearing occasionally during warmer snowfalls along with columns and needles.

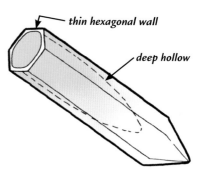

thin hexagonal wall

deep hollow

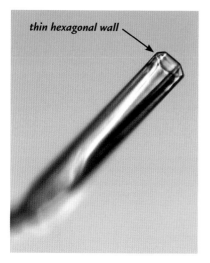

thin hexagonal wall

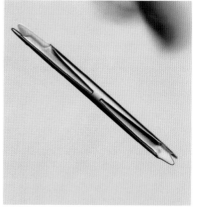

These crystals are another product of the knife-edge instability that promotes the fast growth of thin edges. A sheath starts out like an ordinary hollow column, growing near the usual columnar temperature of –5° C (23° F). But the growth takes off if the conditions are just right to promote the instability. A good specimen will only develop fully when the temperature is optimal and the humidity is high and constant. For some reason, the best sheaths are usually one-sided, as in the photos above and at right, growing from isolated bullet crystals.

Cups

Cups are stout crystals with flared walls that resemble shallow hexagonal goblets. They are similar to capped columns (or capped bullets), except that their caps are not flat plates. Cups are small and quite rare, so they can be difficult to spot. They are typically mixed in with small plates and columns during warmer snowfalls.

Cups are one answer to the question of what types of snow crystals grow when the temperature is between that where columns and plates form. Most cups start out as columns, usually in bullet form, growing near –5° C (23° F). Then the temperature rises or falls a bit, but not quite enough to make capped columns. Instead, the growth flares out into something between a hollow column and a flat plate.

Crystals growing at intermediate temperatures (between plates and columns in the morphology diagram) tend to be stout, blocky, and small. Their low size-to-mass ratio means they remain small even if they accumulate quite a lot of material.

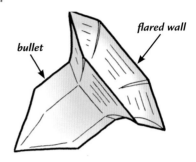

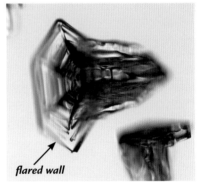

Double-cup crystals (not shown) are made when a simple column develops flared walls on both its ends. Double cups are much less common than single-ended cups growing on bullets.

Bullet rosette with cups

Triangular Crystals

Triangular snow crystals display a three-fold symmetry rather than the usual sixfold symmetry. The most common shape is a truncated triangular plate, sometimes with branching. Triangular crystals are relatively rare and are usually small. They are most likely to be found during warmer snowfalls, mixed in with other small plates and columns.

In spite of outward appearances, triangular snow crystals do not have an abnormal crystal symmetry. Their molecules are still arranged in the usual hexagonal lattice, and the facet angles are unchanged. But while these crystals are growing, for some unknown reason, three prism facets grow faster than the others.

Triangular plates usually form at temperatures near –2° C (28° F). They are inconspicuous and are best found by scanning over lots of small crystals with a microscope.

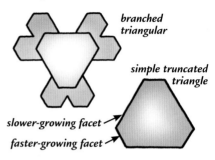

branched triangular

simple truncated triangle

slower-growing facet

faster-growing facet

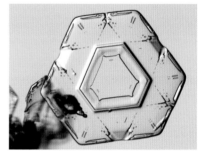

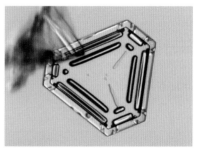

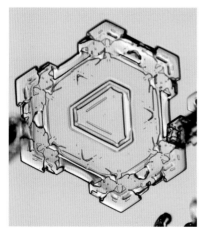

ribs outline initial truncated
triangular plate

branches sprout
from corners

Case Study 37: A Three-Sided Mystery. The prominent ribs on the inner part of this snowflake reveal that it initially grew into a faceted, truncated triangular plate. As it grew larger, branches sprouted and grew out from the six corners. This atypically large specimen is nearly 3 mm (0.1 inches) from tip to tip.

The origin of triangular crystals remains something of a mystery, especially during the early stages of growth that produce relatively simple, truncated triangular plates. We do not know what mechanism causes the six prism facets to grow at different rates. The process is not entirely random, as evidenced by the fact that triangular crystals tend to fall in groups. If you find one, you're likely to find several in the same snowfall.

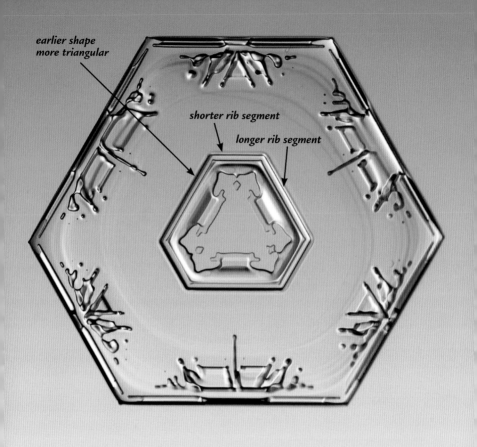

earlier shape more triangular

shorter rib segment

longer rib segment

Case Study 38: A Reformed Triangle. The small plate above adds another twist to the mystery of how triangular crystals grow. Its overall shape looks almost hexagonal, if you consider only its outer edges; the six segments around the perimeter are all nearly the same length. But if you look at the ribs near the center, you can see that the crystal was more triangular when it was small; the longer rib segments are about twice as long as the shorter segments. This means that when the crystal was small, three prism facets grew considerably faster than the other three, which made the crystal triangular. Later on, something happened to make all six facets grow at about the same rate, so the shape became more hexagonal. The mystery is that we cannot say what made the growth change.

I found this specimen in northern Michigan, mixed in with many other hexagonal plates and quite a few triangular ones. Note how the threefold symmetry persists even to the markings around the outer edges of the crystal.

Crystal Twins

A crystal twin is a special polycrystalline form consisting of two separate single-crystal pieces joined together. The pieces are joined in specific orientations, and a few types are common enough that you see them with some regularity. Twins are small and easy to overlook in the midst of other crystals, unless you know to watch for them.

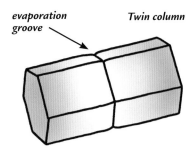

evaporation groove

Twin column

Twin Columns. These look very much like ordinary single-crystal columns, except a twin column has a distinct line, called an *evaporation groove*, running around its middle like a belt. When regular columns are falling in good numbers, you can almost always spot some twins mixed in. To find them, just look for the groove.

To see what a twin column actually is, imagine taking a single-crystal column and slicing it into two half-length columns. Then rotate one piece by 60 degrees, and reattach the two halves. The molecular bonds

would actually fit together pretty well after this operation, although not quite as well as before. If the rotation had been 120 degrees, the reattached bonds would be identical to the original, and equally as strong.

Nature performs this twist accidentally when the crystal is born, and the twin pair grows much like a normal column. But the molecular bonds along the twin plane are a bit weaker than in a single crystal. Sublimation preferentially removes the molecules in this plane, producing the evaporation groove.

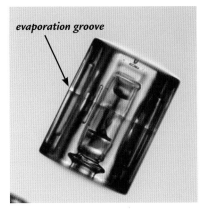

evaporation groove

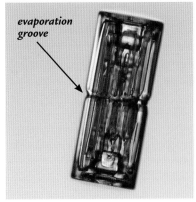

evaporation groove

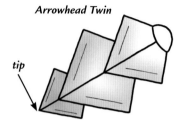

Arrowhead Twin

tip

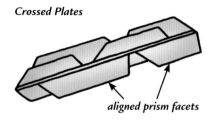

Crossed Plates

aligned prism facets

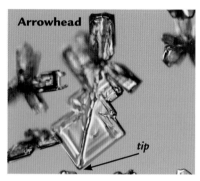

Arrowhead

tip

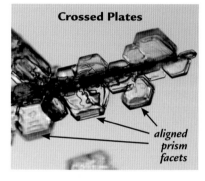

Crossed Plates

aligned prism facets

Arrowhead Twins. Constructions like the above are called *arrowhead crystals* or *Gohei twins*, the latter name coming from similar-looking paper strips hanging at Shinto shrines. These twins come in two varieties—with a 90-degree tip angle (pictured) or with a 79-degree tip angle (sketched). Arrowheads are always accompanied by hollow columns and needles, to which they are often attached.

The two halves of an arrowhead twin are unusual plates that are basically like unwrapped sheaths growing at –5° C (23° F). The flat faces are prism facets and the fast-growing edges are basal facets, which is opposite from normal plates.

Crossed Plates. Plates growing at –2° C (28° F) frequently take the form of a series of crossed plates, shown above. These are crystal twins in which the plates are approximately at right angles to one another, and the prism facets are aligned so their outer edges are parallel.

Crossed plates can be quite abundant, but are nevertheless difficult to recognize and photograph. They form at such high temperatures that sublimation rounds the edges a great deal. Most specimens are so eroded that you can barely make out that they are crossed plates at all. The aligned prism facets are an identifying feature.

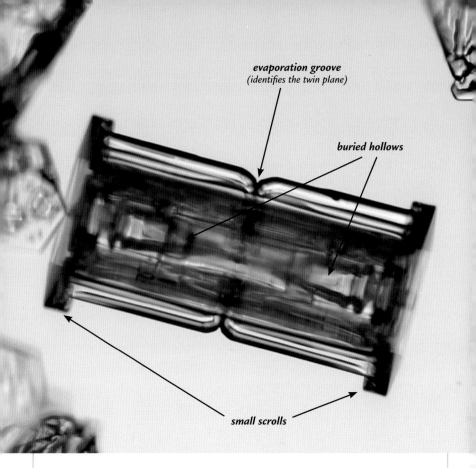

evaporation groove
(identifies the twin plane)

buried hollows

small scrolls

Case Study 39: A Capped Twin Column with Hollows and Scrolls. This example demonstrates several exceptional design features. It has an especially deep evaporation groove, clearly indicating that it's a twin column. You can also see some hollowing inside the column, and small scrolls around the edges of both end plates.

Crystal twins like this one originate during the earliest stages of growth, when the ice nucleus is extremely tiny. As molecules jostle into position to add to the growing lattice, they don't always stack together correctly. Sometimes a defect will form and propagate to produce an entire sheet of defects, which is the twin plane. The process is analogous to buttoning your shirt wrong. If you put the first button in a wrong buttonhole, the mistake propagates and the entire shirt will be buttoned incorrectly. Some stacking faults propagate in much the same way once they get started. Different kinds of defects will do this, and each produces a different type of crystal twin.

Twelve-branched Snowflakes

A twelve-branched snowflake is essentially a matched pair of six-branched stellar crystals attached at their centers, with one rotated 30 degrees relative to the other. This is another polycrystalline form that results from crystal twinning. Twelve-branched snowflakes are rare, but they can occasionally be found mixed in with normal stellar crystals.

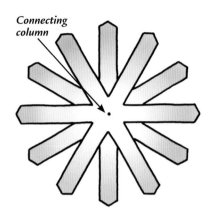

Connecting column

The origin of twelve-branched snowflakes has never been properly explained. They occur rarely, but not randomly. Most snowfalls produce none that you can find. But if you spot one, you're likely to see several on the same day. Twelve-branched snowflakes are created when conditions are just right, but we don't yet know what conditions cause them to occur.

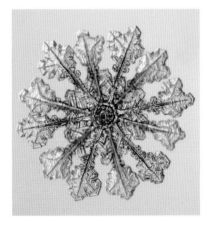

Case Study 40: Capped Column with a Twist. Each twelve-branched snow-flake is really a pair of six-branched crystals separated by a twinned column. The central column is essentially the same as the twin columns described previously, except with a 30-degree twist instead of a 60-degree twist. Starting from such a twin, the crystal then develops into a double plate with two sets of arms. This is the mechanism by which an ice crystal can form what looks like a twelve-fold-symmetrical structure.

For most twelve-branched snowflakes, the initial column is short, but in the example above it is unusually long. Thus the two stellar plates are sufficiently separated that my microscope could distinguish them by refocusing. This specimen fell one day along with a great many well-formed capped columns of the ordinary variety.

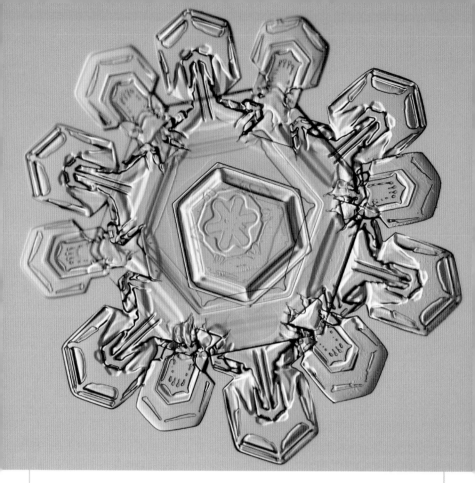

Case Study 41: Accidental Twelve. How do we know that a twelve-branched snowflake is not just two independent six-branched crystals that collided and stuck together? Well, if the two plates are off-center relative to one another, then the assembly probably is the result of a chance collision. The above photograph, for example, shows two stellar plates that almost certainly formed separately and then collided. Another indication of this is that we see no central column connecting the two crystals.

Even if the two parts are rather aligned, you still cannot say for sure by looking at just one specimen. Even chance collisions can occasionally produce a well-aligned pair. But if you look at a lot of twelve-branched snowflakes, you find a sizable fraction with their two sides nearly perfectly oriented, and these tend to appear in groups. From these observations, we can conclude that not all twelve-branched snowflakes are produced by random collisions, and that most are real crystal twins.

Irregular Snowflakes

Irregular snowflakes are small, poorly formed crystals with little discernable symmetry. They look like fragments of plates, columns, and intermediate forms, often sublimated and clumped together. Irregulars are by far the most common snow crystal type, and they are abundant during every snowfall.

If you examine a random sampling of falling snow, say by looking at everything that lands on a glass slide, you will typically find that the majority of crystals are irregulars. For too many snowfalls, the fraction is close to 100 percent. These crystals form under nonideal conditions, with growth impeded by crowding from neighbors, crystal defects, midair collisions, sublimation, and any number of other problems.

I also call these *granular snowflakes* because they look like grains of white, fluffy sand on your sleeve, with none of the sparkle of larger, faceted crystals.

Hoarfrost

Hoarfrost is made of ice crystals that have many of the same forms as snow crystals, including faceted and branched plates, dendrites, and hollow columns. Hoarfrost is found on plants or other surfaces near ground level, and on the tops of snowbanks. Hoarfrost crystals are frequently much larger than snow crystals, making their structure easily visible with the naked eye.

Frost appears when water vapor condenses from the air to form ice crystals on the ground. The freezing process is essentially the same as for snow crystals, and thus produces similar structures. When the crystals are tiny, they are just called frost. When the crystals grow larger, so faceting and branching are apparent, then the name changes to hoarfrost.

Hoarfrost crystals on the surfaces of snowbanks are especially common. If you see a lot of sparkle coming from a snowbank in the sun, especially in the early morning, you are most likely seeing reflections from the facets of hoarfrost crystals. These form after sunset, when the air temperature quickly drops but the snowbank still retains some of its daytime warmth. The temperature difference drives water vapor from the warmer depths to condense on the colder surface, forming a layer of new hoarfrost crystals overnight.

Hoarfrost crystals growing on a plant

dendrite branch

Part III

OBSERVING
SNOWFLAKES

Magnification

Because snowflakes are small, you need some optical gear in order to identify and examine different crystals. The available options range from inexpensive magnifiers to fancy microscopes, depending on your level of interest and your budget.

The place to start is with a basic magnifying lens, which you can find for just a few dollars at most drugstores and hardware stores. These give a surprisingly good view, and the fold-up models are compact and light enough to carry in your coat pocket or glove compartment.

Keeping a magnifier handy, preferably in your coat pocket, is essential for good snowflake watching. Each snowfall is different, and you cannot always find nice crystals. The best strategy is to take a quick look whenever you see it snowing. This could be while skiing or snowmobiling, or perhaps by just looking outside your front door. If you see some interesting crystals, get out your magnifier and have a closer look. The key to finding great snowflakes is to always be on the lookout.

A jeweler's loupe is a somewhat higher-quality viewing option. A good loupe costs about $30 and has better optical quality than less-expensive magnifiers. A 7X loupe is good for most snowflake viewing, but you may also want a 10X loupe to examine smaller crystals.

The best instrument for snowflake watching is a microscope. Even an inexpensive model can cost $150, but it will provide a much more detailed view than any simple magnifier. If you want to see detail, then you ought to take the plunge and invest in a microscope. Snowflakes can be truly breathtaking when you see them for yourself at high magnification.

You can find more information about snowflake-watching gear, including a buyer's guide to magnifiers, loupes, and microscopes, at my website: *www.snowcrystals.com.*

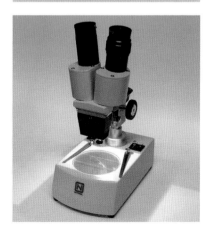

inexpensive plastic magnifier

jeweler's loupe

Snowflake Photography

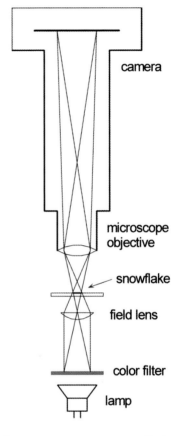

camera

microscope objective

snowflake

field lens

color filter

lamp

Capturing detailed images of snowflakes presents some unique challenges to a photographer. The crystals are small, they can be tricky to handle, and, of course, you must work outside in below-freezing temperatures. Nevertheless, snowflake photography can be great fun if you're so inclined, and it's not especially difficult if you use the right equipment and methods. With some effort and perseverance, together with a sufficiently cold climate, anyone can put together a collection of beautiful snowflake pictures.

If you would like to try your hand at snowflake photography, I recommend building a setup like that shown in the diagram at right (for clarity, not all parts are drawn to scale). This is what I used to take the photographs in this book, and I believe the overall layout is optimal for the task. I'll warn you from the outset that building your own snowflake microscope is more than a one-weekend project, but it's doable if you're willing to try and you're not afraid of a little tinkering.

Starting from the top of the diagram, nearly any camera with a removable lens should work. I prefer a digital SLR model because I take a lot of pictures and because digital photographs are convenient and generally less grainy than film.

Regardless of your choice of camera, it must be kept at above-freezing temperature at all times. Even rugged models are usually not designed to be operated at, or even stored at, low temperatures. Also, you should not bring a cold camera into a warm house, since condensation might cause damage. I keep my camera inside a simple styrofoam box, along with a five-watt heater that keeps it warm and functional in even the coldest conditions.

Moving down the diagram, a quality *microscope objective* is a must. My favorite is the Mitutoyo M Plan Apo 5X objective, available at Edmund Optics for about $500. Less-expensive objectives are available, and these probably produce good pictures as well. It's generally true in photography that more expensive lenses deliver better pictures, but often your lens is not the limiting factor, so it's hard to know how much to spend.

The Mitutoyo 5X has a *numerical aperture* (N.A.) of 0.14, which is a good choice for snowflakes. A lower N.A. has lower resolution and will not produce bitingly sharp images. A higher N.A. has better resolution but such a low depth of field that it cannot hold focus on all parts of a snow crystal. In microscopy, there is always a trade-off between resolution and depth of field, so choosing the right numerical aperture is important.

Once you have a microscope objective, the magnification is then set by the distance between it and the camera. The greater the distance, the higher the magnification and the smaller the field of view. I use extension tubes to set up my 5X with a field of view of about 3 mm (0.12 inches), which is good for medium-sized crystals. I also use the 2X and 10X Mitutoyo objectives for larger and smaller crystals, respectively, but I find the 5X always gets the most use.

Focusing is accomplished by moving the snowflake up and down using a *translation stage*. You could instead move the objective, but with microscopes it is usually easier to move the stage.

For illumination, I recommend the combination of a *field lens* and *color filter* shown in the diagram. With this arrangement, the field lens focuses the filter onto the microscope objective (i.e., the pupil), which provides for all sorts of interesting color play while providing a uniform background. Using filters with different patterns accentuates the crystal structure, as is described in more detail below.

The final challenge in this setup is to hold the various parts together. The camera, microscope objective, translation stage, and lighting hardware all need to be securely mounted. Edmund Optics is a good place for parts, and there are many possible options. A little trial and error is usually required at this point to get it all working. Fortunately, it need not be done outside in the cold. Small bits of plastic make fine surrogate snowflakes for testing photo quality.

More details about making your own snowflake photo-microscope can also be found at *www.snowcrystals.com*.

Finding Snowflakes

Finding and handling snowflakes is another challenge. Nice crystals are often inconspicuous, plus they are somewhat fragile and are easily damaged by heat. Different collecting techniques are useful under different conditions, depending on the temperature and what types of snowflakes are falling.

When photographing larger varieties, such as stellar plates and dendrites, start by letting some snowflakes fall onto a dark-colored collecting board. Scan the surface as they fall, looking for interesting subjects. Well-formed, symmetrical plates are always great to find, but keep a lookout for exotic specimens as well.

When a promising subject appears, carefully pick it up using a small artist's paintbrush, and place it on a glass microscope slide. The crystals stick to the brush surprisingly well, without suffering much damage, so the transfer is easier than you might think. If the brush isn't working, use a sharpened toothpick as diminutive shovel. After moving the crystal onto the slide, put it under the microscope to be photographed.

Speed is important once a snowflake is under the lights, since the additional heat causes increased sublimation. This problem is much worse at higher temperatures, giving you little time to adjust the microscope for a good shot.

The author with his traveling snowflake microscope, in search of the perfect snowflake. Photograph by Rachel Wing

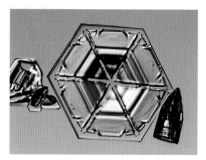

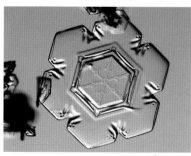

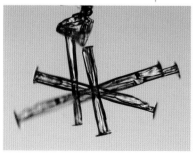

When smaller snowflakes are falling, as is typically the case on warmer days, using a collecting board becomes impractical. The interesting specimens are difficult to pick out and are even more difficult to pick up. Then it's time to switch to catching crystals directly on microscope slides.

Start by spreading out several cold slides on your collecting board, supporting them by the edges to keep their bottom surfaces clean. When a slide has a nice dusting of new snow, place it under the microscope and scan back and forth for nice crystals. Once you've seen what one slide has to offer, wipe it off, set it out to collect more, and try another.

This simple strategy is surprisingly effective, and it is about the only viable method I have found for photographing small crystals. Nearly all my pictures of diamond dust crystals, hollow columns, needles, and bullet rosettes were taken this way. Some examples are shown on the left. Even when you see little that seems worthy of a closer look on your sleeve, you can usually find something interesting under the microscope.

Remember that the character of a snowfall can change from hour to hour, even with rather subtle changes in temperature or in other conditions. If you want to find great snow crystals, you have to keep watching.

Lighting

What a snow crystal looks like depends a great deal on how it is illuminated. Reflection and refraction are both important in snowflake photography, and both can be exploited in different ways to produce a variety of colorful effects.

The diagram at right shows three basic illumination techniques. The first, *transmitted light*, uses multicolored light shining up though the snow crystal from below. The curved ice surface then acts like a very complex lens to refract the incident light in interesting ways.

The color in a snowflake photograph is determined by the colored lights you use. For example, the photograph below was taken using transmitted light like that shown in the diagram (upper right). Some parts of the crystal refract the light to the right, and those areas show up with subtle red highlights. Other parts bend the light to the left, and those areas show blue highlights. Edges that refract the light through large angles appear dark. The background includes contributions from all incident angles, so it is intermediate in both color and brightness.

By using different colors and shades, transmitted light is especially good at revealing the inner structure of snow crystals.

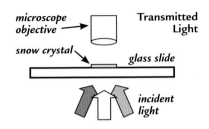

Transmitted Light

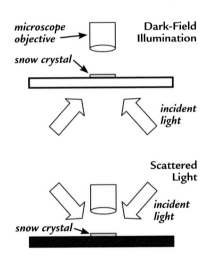

Dark-Field Illumination

Scattered Light

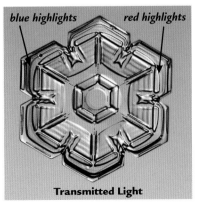

Transmitted Light

Dark-Field Illumination

Scattered Light

The second technique, *dark-field illumination*, gives snowflakes a very different look. The top picture above shows the same crystal as before, except using the dark-field method. Using this technique, light is incident from below at very steep angles. If nothing refracts or scatters the light, then none enters the microscope objective. Thus, the background is dark,

as are smooth areas of the crystal. Edges scatter light into the microscope and appear to shimmer brightly against the dark background.

The same optical layout used for transmitted light can also produce dark-field images. You simply use a filter with a large, opaque spot in the center, so that only oblique illumination is incident on the crystal.

Sometimes I use a filter with a dark-colored (but not quite opaque) center and a variety of colors around the sides, which combines aspects of transmitted light and dark-field illumination to yield different, colorful effects. The photograph on page 46 is an example using this intermediate method.

The third technique, *scattered light*, is how you see a snowflake on your sleeve. The second picture at left was taken using this method, with the crystal on an opaque surface. This shot required a different optical layout from the previous two, since light had to shine down on the crystal from above. In this picture, you can see the accentuated edges, and you can see how the background surface is visible through clear parts of the ice. If the crystal had been placed on a transparent surface, then the picture would have looked similar to a dark-field image. In general, I find scattered light delivers the least appealing snowflake photographs, so I rarely use this method.

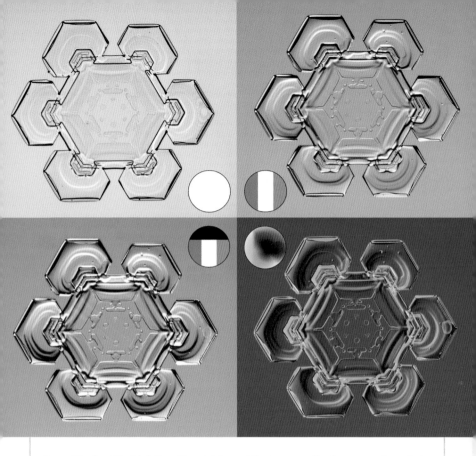

Case Study 42: Lighting Comparison. These are all photographs of the same snow crystal taken using different lighting. Each used the optical layout shown on page 103, with the different color filters shown next to each image.

The plain filter (upper left) produces a rather "flat" image that fails to show the internal structure of the crystal with much detail. This unsatisfactory result is what you often get if you simply shine some light through a crystal without paying a lot of attention to technique. The red/white/blue filter (upper right) produces considerably more depth, along with some colorful highlights around the edges of the crystal. The red/white/blue/black filter (lower left) accentuates the crystal structure further and gives the image an even greater sense of depth. The rainbow filter (lower right) provides something similar to dark-field illumination, but with a dark blue background and a variety of color highlights decorating the different crystal edges. With additional patterned filters, you can produce an endless variety of colorful lighting effects.

Case Study 43: Opaque Background. I took this picture using scattered light, with the snow crystal placed on a small piece of a paper that had been printed using an ink-jet printer. The paper had a uniform reddish grey color to the eye, but appeared mottled under the microscope, which gave the background a pleasing texture. Note how clear many portions of the crystal are, especially around the center and in the sectored-plate arms.

Case Study 44: Winter's Secret Beauty. Snow crystals are wonderful examples of nature's art, even as they are wrapped in the cold winds and dreary skies of winter. When you stop to notice them, snowflakes are a delight to find on your sleeve and are absolutely fascinating when viewed under a microscope. Their complex structures grow and develop as they tumble through the clouds, each design ephemeral and never again to be exactly repeated.

Don't be satisfied just gazing at these photographs. Get your magnifier and venture outside during the next snowfall. Witness firsthand these dimunitive ice masterpieces. You may be amazed by what you find.

Index

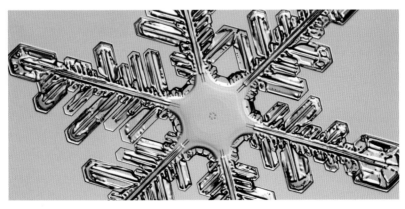